Governmental Budgeting Workbook

Bridging Theory and Practice

Third Edition

David L. Baker
Marc K. Fudge
Alexandru V. Roman

California State University,
San Bernardino

Copyright © 2015 by Birkdale Publishers, Inc.
2 3 4 5 6 7 8 9 10

Cover by Erika Shiroma

ISBN 978-1-942456-00-1

Birkdale Publishers, Inc.
P.O. Box 270261
San Diego, CA 92198-0261
website   www.BirkdalePublishers.com
telephone   858 774 6075

Contents

Preface

David Baker conceived of and developed the first *Governmental Budgeting Workbook* and added new material in the second edition. This third edition adds two colleagues, Marc Fudge and Alexandru Roman as co-authors. They have enriched the usefulness of material presented and supplied the two new case studies. Their substantive contributions extend the value of the *Workbook* while ensuring its future for many more years. Together, we are pleased to contribute the *Workbook* to complement and to support student learning about governmental budgeting. We believe in governmental excellence, with efficient, economic, and effective service delivery bounded by exemplary ethics and dedicated to public service values. Our intent was to create a workbook which takes a hands-on approach to governmental budgeting that reflects the perspective of practitioners. Nonetheless, we believe that "doing" governmental budgeting well also requires a strong theoretical and conceptual understanding of the discipline.

Thoroughly updated to reflect current budget realities, the third edition of the Governmental Budgeting Workbook drops one exercise from the previous edition while, adding two new case studies. One covers budgetary obligations and their cumulative nature in financial management decisions, especially when an overly influential leader is involved. The other exposes students to the numerous and complex issues that result from unethical decision-making. The Workbook aims to hone the analytical skills today's complex budgeting requires through student-centered exercises. The exercises engage critical thinking skills while anchoring theory with realistic applications. They strive to bridge the gap between budgetary theory and practice and give a real-world "feel" for budgeting. The exercises are flexible enough to support many different textbooks and approaches to this fascinating and essential skill area for aspiring and in-service public employees.

In working on the third edition, we have benefited from the thoughtful suggestions, comments, and constructive criticisms of the following reviewers:

John Bohte, University of Wisconsin, Milwaukee

Natalia Ermasova, Governors State University

Marcus D. Mauldin, University of Tennessee, Chattanooga

Agustin León-Moreta, University of New Mexico

Megan Streams, Tennessee State University

This workbook is dedicated to you, the student. It is our hope that it supports you in a successful career in public service. It also is dedicated to Dean Karen Dill Bowerman (Retired), College of Business and Public Administration, California State University, San Bernardino who enthusiastically encouraged the development of the original edition. We shall be forever grateful to her.

David L. Baker   Marc K. Fudge   Alexandru V. Roman

California State University, San Bernardino

October 2014

Exercise 1

Precourse Governmental Budgeting Student Survey

Learning Objectives:

 To engage you in identifying and exploring your current level of knowedge about governmental budgeting.

 To stimulate your interest in the course content by raising course-related questions.

Background

For many of you, this course in governmental budgeting is your first exposure to public agency budgets. Those with some knowledge about governmental budgeting can be identified through this survey and called upon to share their insights during class. For those with little knowledge about governmental budgeting, this survey can help stimulate your interest and foreshadow future learning in this subject. The precourse survey may be revisited after the postcourse survey is taken during one of the last course sessions. This permits you to reflect on what you have learned through the course.

Assignment

Complete the Precourse Governmental Budgeting Student Survey on pages 3–5.

Name _____ Date _____

Precourse Governmental Budgeting Student Survey

Although this is an ungraded assignment, please complete the following survey as comprehensively as possible.

1. What classes in public administration or related fields have you already taken?

   _____

   _____

   _____

2. What public agency internship or employment experience have you had? (Identify the agency and job title, and briefly describe the job responsibilities.)

   _____

   _____

   _____

   _____

3. What other internships or employment have you had?

   _____

   _____

   _____

   _____

4. List the governmental budgets with which you have come in contact.

   _____

   _____

   _____

   _____

5. Explain your current understanding of governmental budgeting. What is a budget? Why do public agencies prepare them? Why should citizens be concerned with governmental budgets?

_____

_____

_____

_____

_____

_____

6. How do you see governmental budgeting impacting the economy?

_____

_____

_____

_____

7. What terms or concepts are you aware of that have to do with a typical governmental budget cycle?

_____

_____

_____

_____

_____

_____

_____

8. Briefly describe at least three common approaches to developing governmental budgets.

_____

_____

_____

_____

_____

_____

9. Briefly describe ways a governmental budget may be modified once adopted?

_____

_____

_____

_____

Exercise 2

A Case Study in Budgetary Ethics

Learning Objectives:

☑ To sharpen critical thinking skills by examining a real-life inspired case study.

☑ To expose you to the numerous and complex issues that result from unethical decision-making.

☑ To introduce you to the subtle differences between illegal and unethical decisions.

☑ To develop a course of action that provides a road map to addressing the problems caused by unethical decisions.

Background

Copper Springs is a scenic and picturesque city of approximately 190,000 people. It is located 30 minutes north of Big Town, a more densely populated city that has nearly one million residents. The residents of Copper Springs enjoy its relative tranquility, sprawling landscapes, and the residential suburban feel. With its close proximity to the neighboring metropolis, it is an easy commute to regional employers. For the past several years Copper Springs has seen a steady increase in the number of new residents who are looking to get away from the hustle and bustle of big city life.

The economic conditions in Copper Springs have traditionally been favorable. Even after the recent downturn in the economy, the city did not have to resort to any departmental contractions or layoffs. In fact, annual city revenues averaged a three percent increase over the past five years.

Copper Springs uses a strong mayor-council form of government. The mayor is elected separately from the council and serves as the chief executive officer in overseeing daily administrative operations. Contingent upon council confirmation, the position appoints and removes department heads. While the council has legislative power, the mayor has veto power.

Nathan Turnicott is the new mayor of Copper Springs starting his third year in office and planning to run for re-election. He formerly worked in the Big Town City Attorney's Office as a Chief Deputy City Attorney. He earned notoriety for winning several high profile cases involving shady land development issues where ties to an organized crime syndicate were suspected. Turnicott was known to be tough, a straight-shooter, and having a "no holds barred" approach. He succeeded the very popular Eldwin Archer who served for four terms. The personable and charismatic Archer likely would have run for re-election had it not been for new state legislation establishing term limits for mayors. Although not a native to Copper Springs, most residents felt as if Turnicott was aptly suited to succeed Archer and manage their city.

One of the main initiatives Mayor Turnicott undertook in his first year was the development and implementation of a performance management system to help the city run more efficiently. Following the success of the Office of Performance Management within Big Town, he championed the creation of a similar unit in Copper Springs. Primarily relying upon approximately a one million dollar increase in sales tax revenue from the previous year, Mayor Turnicott had the necessary funds to create a new governmental unit. Approved by a slim majority from the city council, Copper Springs created the Office of Performance Improvement (OPI). The objectives of the OPI in Copper Springs are to improve governmental accountability, enhance transparency, and facilitate strong citizen participation. Furthermore, the mayor is a big proponent of technology and using data to inform decision-making. He strongly believes that an office like OPI will be seen as a "hallmark" for the city. Ultimately, Mayor Turnicott would like to implement a performance-based budgeting system to help the city run more efficiently.

The new office has a staff of seven that includes a director, one assistant director, four administrative analysts and one administrative assistant. The new office space for OPI, staff salaries and benefits, along with the necessary computer and office equipment, has cost the city nearly $900,000. Included in budgetary expenditures of OPI is a state of the art website that allows residents to view and conduct queries of performance data online. While $900,000 only represents about .3% of Copper Springs' current annual budget of roughly $304,000,000, it represents 1.25% of the city's discretionary $71,744,000 general fund. Some city council members are concerned because OPI's operating expenses are likely to continue to increase and there is no guarantee that it will save the city money in the future. One member of the city council who opposed the creation of OPI said that the money should be put to better use, while another stated that the new mayor was "raiding the coffers for something that may, or may not be effective." Ultimately, Turnicott aims for the city to move to a performance budgeting system and he believes that the return on investment from the initial cost of OPI will prove to be beneficial in just a few short years. As he sees it, "We need to invest in our future now and the best time to save money, is when you have money."

While the population has continued to increase in Copper Springs, the number of sworn police officers has slightly decreased. Now officers are asked to work longer hours to cover the community effectively. Nearly all officers are willing to work overtime because of the extra pay. However, extending officer shifts introduces certain problems such as officer fatigue. Another related issue is the increased use of sick time which further depletes the police department's limited resources. Additionally, the police department is in need of new safety equipment, radios and video cameras for patrol staff. As these issues continue to grow within the police department there has been a simultaneous increase in crime. Most city managers and even some astute citizens seem to believe that the ratio of growing population to officers is out of whack and a reason for concern in Copper Springs.

Recently, one of the administrative analysts within OPI was analyzing data from the police department. She noticed that 911 response times to crimes have significantly increased over the past three months from four minutes, ten seconds to more than seven minutes. The Data Submittal Form signed by the police chief notes that "due to a decline in personnel, 911 response times have slightly increased." She raises her concerns with the assistant director because, in her opinion, the increase in 911 response times is not slight. The assistant director discusses the issue with the director of OPI and she immediately contacts mayor Turnicott. Mayor Turnicott states "This is interesting. Let's see what happens next month. It could be an aberration." The director tells her staff to monitor the situation closely for another month to see how the situation plays out.

The following month 911 response times have increased again, from over seven minutes to nearly 10 minutes. The director of OPI once again contacts the mayor to relay the bad news. The news grabs the mayor's attention as he struggles with mixed feelings. On the one hand, this could be considered as good news. This data validates the importance of performance indicators and the wisdom behind creating OPI to monitor performance data independently as it is reported. Without OPI, this increase in 911 response times may have gone unnoticed for months or not reviewed until budgets are compiled again. On the other hand, Mayor Turnicott is upset. Not only has he no explanation for the problem, he knows that once the residents notice the spike, he will be held partially responsible. He contacts the chief of police with whom he has a good relationship and asks why there is an increase in 911 response times. The police chief is aware of the increase in response times and simply states, "The department needs more officers." Mayor Turnicott tells the chief he'll do what he can, but there is no money in the budget to hire more officers this year. Mayor Turnicott also knows that there may not be money in next year's budget because OPI continues to drain city resources. Furthermore, the mayor knows that if he reduces OPI staff, or eliminates it altogether, his innovative initiative will look like a failure and, undoubtedly, this could have a major negative impact on his bid for re-election. The mayor is hesitant to wait another month to see what the police data will show. He sets up a meeting with the director of OPI and "suggests" that it would be "really great" to "come up" with some "data or report" that would show how much the performance of the city administration has improved since the OPI started its operations. The mayor even has a number in mind.

He believes that the report should show at least $1,000,000 in savings. After noticing the director's quizzical look, the mayor tells her that 911 response times "must" decrease next month. The director says that she cannot simply make the numbers go down, but the mayor insists. "If they do not go down, you'll be looking for another job."

The director is now clearly worried. She did not accept this position to be bullied or to manipulate data. She wants to present accurate and authentic data but she also wants to keep her job. Begrudgingly she secretly tells the administrative analyst who monitors the police department's data to make the response rate numbers go down. She also reflects on the differences between illegal and unethical actions. Legal actions deal with what is permitted or authorized by law while illegal are those actions that are prohibited by law. Ethical refers to judgments about right and wrong guided by principles. She decides to review the International City/County Manager Association's (ICMA) Code of Ethics which she finds on the ICMA website (http://icma.org/en/icma/home). Additionally, she will seek the city attorney's advice regarding legal provisions related to collection and dissemination of departmental performance data.

When the following month's police data are made available on OPIs website, the police chief notices that 911 response times have surprisingly decreased. He realizes that this information is incorrect because of the Data Submittal Form he previously signed. He also knows that it is impossible because of the increased number of complaints he has received from citizens regarding the length of time it takes officers to arrive at a scene. Despite what he knows, he does not rock the boat by contacting OPI or the mayor.

Mayor Turnicott also has received complaints regarding 911 response times and he directs those to the OPI website where, after a brief spike, police response times have decreased. During this time, a woman is severely beaten by her boyfriend and nearly dies as a result of her injuries. Neighbors say that it took the police at least 15 minutes to respond to the initial 911 call. In an effort to defuse the situation, the mayor decides to begin commenting on the Copper Spring's social media websites. Using a pseudonym, he writes several messages and posts pictures that offer positive commentary about Copper Springs city government. He focuses the majority of his posts on the police department and how good of a job they are doing, in particular the time it takes them to respond to crimes.

The administrative analyst from OPI who had been told to manipulate the police data surmises that the true authorships of the social media messages and pictures are fictitious. She also feels really bad about the case of the battered woman. She dreads saying anything to the director of OPI because of the instructions she was previously given. The analyst cannot be fired as an at-will employer. Yet she fears not following direction will impact her next employee performance evaluation, places the director in a difficult position, and could jeopardize future funding of the continuation of OPI. However, she has decided to decline to manipulate the police data to make it appear more favorable. She will tell the director in writing that she declines to change the police data and leaves the matter to the director for resolution.

Assignment

After carefully reading the case study, answer the questions that follow. Your instructor will indicate whether you should work individually or in groups. While you will be able to derive the answers to some of the questions directly from the reading or the ICMA Code of Ethics, others will require critical thinking. You should note that since this is a case study several questions will not have "correct" answers. Although there are common lessons that everyone can learn from this case, there also can be a diverse set of perspectives when it comes to ethical considerations in the public budgeting process.

Name (group) _____   Date _____

Case Study Assignment Sheets

1. What are the ethical and budgetary developments leading to the issues or problems in the case?

_____

_____

_____

_____

_____

_____

_____

_____

_____

_____

_____

_____

2. Who are the main internal and external stakeholders, and what are their respective interests?

_____

_____

_____

_____

_____

_____

3. Identify the organizational actors who have made questionable ethical decisions.

_____

_____

_____

_____

_____

_____

4. Which internal stakeholders need to make a decision about what they will do going forward?

_____

_____

_____

_____

_____

_____

5. Notwithstanding the actions of the mayor, how could this situation have been avoided?

_____

_____

_____

_____

_____

_____

_____

_____

_____

_____

_____

_____

_____

_____

6. What is likely to occur if the data continues to be manipulated and the public does not become aware of the situation?

_____

_____

_____

_____

_____

_____

7. What impact has the budgeting decisions, made by the mayor (and the city council), had on the issues raised in this case?

_____

_____

_____

_____

_____

_____

8. Assume that you are the director of finance for Copper Springs. After you have been made aware of the mayor's actions and the manipulation of data, what budgetary recommendations do you make regarding OPI? Discuss your recommended course of action.

_____

_____

_____

_____

_____

_____

_____

_____

_____

_____

_____

_____

_____

_____

_____

Exercise 3

Exploring Governmental Budgeting Online

Learning Objectives:

☑ To acquaint you with the relative accessibility and the scope of governmental budget information available through the Internet.

☑ To expose you to various levels of governmental budgeting that have significance to the region in which you live.

☑ To display several budgeting formats and to engage you in thinking about the scope of information provided in online budget documents.

☑ To engage you in evaluating the relative user-friendliness of various online budget information from an interested citizen's perspective.

☑ To develop critical thinking skills in evaluating governmental budgeting information available through the Internet.

Background

Over the past two decades, most public agencies have developed an Internet presence. These websites provide an important venue for disseminating budgeting information and vary considerably in their user-friendliness, content, and sophistication. The Governmental Finance Officers Association (http://www.gfoa.org/) recommends the timely presentation of governmental financial documents to demonstrate transparency and accountability as a "best practice." The key benefits of website presentation include:

- Reaching potential users who can access the information only through the Internet

- Offering information to a wide audience without charge

- Increasing opportunities for agency and user interaction

- Facilitating the possibility of providing financial information in diverse languages

- Enabling users to analyze data electronically

- Promoting the efficiency of a one-stop venue for public financial information

- Economizing on reproduction and distribution costs

- Reducing paper consumption

- Making possible the efficient retrieval of related information through hyperlinks

Assignment

You are to go online individually to access and explore the budget documents of four governmental agencies as indicated below and to then complete the Exploring Governmental Budgeting Online Assignment Sheets.

1. **United State Federal Government**

   Budgetary documents for the federal government can be accessed through the Office of Management and Budget at http://www.whitehouse.gov/omb

2. **Your resident state**

   State websites normally may be found by entering the name of the state and looking for the state's official website (e.g., State of Texas). Alternatively, USA.gov website may provide a route to your state. Go to http://www.usa.gov/Agencies/State-and-Territories.shtml then click on the state in which you are interested.

3. **Your resident county, borough, or parish**

   County, Borough, or Parish websites normally may be found by entering the name of the jurisdiction and looking for the official website (e.g., Maricopa County, Queens Borough, Rapides Parish). Alternatively, the National Association of Counties website provides links to most counties, boroughs, and parishes. Go to http://www.naco. org/. Under "About Counties," click "County Search," then click the state map for a specific jurisdiction, then click on the jurisdiction's name, and go to the official website.

   Not all local governments have websites or a particular website may be temporarily inoperable. If you cannot locate the website you seek after reasonable exploration, document your search attempt and locate another comparable local government website for analysis.

4. **Your resident city or nearest major city**

   City and Town websites normally may be found by entering the name of the city and looking for the city's official website (e.g., City of Seattle). Not all city governments have websites or a particular website may be temporarily inoperable. If you cannot locate the website you seek after reasonable exploration, document your search attempt and locate another comparable local government website for analysis.

Name _____   Date _____

Exploring Governmental Budgeting Online Assignment Sheets

Federal Government

After a general review of the federal government's website, search for available information about the federal budget. Respond to the following questions in your own words.

1. What are the major issues discussed in the budget message?

_____

_____

_____

_____

_____

_____

_____

_____

_____

_____

2. What is the scope of information (e.g., types of information, level of detail, and breadth of coverage regarding federal operations) on the website that relates to the overall budget?

_____

_____

_____

_____

_____

_____

_____

_____

_____

22

Department or Agency _____

URL _____

3. Choose and locate a specific federal agency or department of interest. Please note the department or agency as well and the URL above. Please describe the budget information available about the agency or department with specific details in your words.

_____

_____

_____

_____

_____

_____

_____

_____

_____

_____

4. What is your critique of the federal government's attempt to disclose budget information from an interested citizen's perspective?

_____

_____

_____

_____

_____

_____

_____

_____

_____

_____

State Government

State Name _____

URL _____

After a general review of your state's website, search for available information about your state's budget. Note your state's name and URL above, and respond to the following questions in your own words.

1. What are the major issues discussed in the budget message or overview?

_____

_____

_____

_____

_____

_____

_____

_____

_____

_____

2. What is the scope of state budget information (e.g., types of information, level of detail, and breadth of coverage regarding state operations) on the website that relates to the overall budget?

_____

_____

_____

_____

_____

_____

_____

_____

_____

Department or Agency   _____

URL   _____

Choose and locate a specific agency or department of interest in your state government. Note the department or agency as well as the URL above. Please respond to the following questions in your own words.

3. Describe the budget information available about that agency or department with specific details in your words.

_____

_____

_____

_____

_____

_____

_____

_____

_____

_____

4. What is your critique of the jurisdiction's attempt to disclose budget information from an interested citizen's perspective?

_____

_____

_____

_____

_____

_____

_____

_____

_____

_____

Local (County Level) Government

Name and type of local jurisdiction _____

URL _____

After a general review of your county, borough, or parish's website, search for available budget information about the jurisdiction. Note the name of your local governing body and URL above. Please respond to the following questions in your own words.

1. What are the major issues discussed in the budget message or overview?

_____

_____

_____

_____

_____

_____

_____

_____

_____

_____

2. What is the scope of the jurisdiction's budget information (e.g., types of information, level of detail, and breadth of coverage regarding the jurisdiction's operations) on the website that relates to the overall budget?

_____

_____

_____

_____

_____

_____

_____

_____

_____

_____

Department or Agency   _____

URL   _____

Choose and locate a specific agency or department of interest in your local government. Note the department or agency as well and the URL above. Please respond to the following questions in your own words.

3. Describe the budget information available about that agency or department with specific details in your words.

_____

_____

_____

_____

_____

_____

_____

_____

_____

_____

4. What is your critique of the jurisdiction's attempt to disclose budget information from an interested citizen's perspective?

_____

_____

_____

_____

_____

_____

_____

_____

_____

_____

_____

City Government

City Name _____

URL _____

After a general review of your city government's website, search for available information about your city's budget. Note your city's name and URL above and respond to the following questions in your own words.

1. What are the major issues discussed in the budget message or overview?

_____

_____

_____

_____

_____

_____

_____

_____

_____

_____

2. What is the scope of the jurisdiction's budget information (e.g., types of information, level of detail, and breadth of coverage regarding the jurisdiction's operations) on the website that relates to the overall budget?

_____

_____

_____

_____

_____

_____

_____

_____

_____

Department or Agency   _____

URL   _____

Choose and locate a specific agency or department of interest in your city government. Note the department or agency as well and the URL above. Please respond to the following questions in your own words.

3. Describe the budget information available about that agency or department with specific details in your words.

_____

_____

_____

_____

_____

_____

_____

_____

_____

_____

4. What is your critique of the jurisdiction's attempt to disclose budget information from an interested citizen's perspective?

_____

_____

_____

_____

_____

_____

_____

_____

_____

Debriefing Analysis and Discussion

1. Based on your review of the four government levels, compare and contrast what you found most useful and most in need of improvement about the online budget information from an interested citizen's perspective.

_____

_____

_____

_____

_____

_____

_____

_____

_____

2. If you assume that your boss assigned you to perform a detailed analysis of one of these jurisdiction's budgets, what additional information would you seek for each jurisdiction and why?

Federal Government

_____

_____

_____

_____

State Government

_____

_____

_____

_____

Local Government

_____

_____

_____

_____

City Government

_____

_____

_____

_____

3. What do you see as the challenges and opportunities of Internet-based governmental budgeting information?

_____

_____

_____

_____

_____

_____

_____

_____

_____

_____

Exercise 4

GFOA Website's Best Practices

Learning Objectives:

☑ To acquaint you with the background supporting *Best Practices* available through the Government Finance Officers' Association (GFOA) website at http://www.gfoa.org/.

☑ To familiarize you with the broad GFOA categories and specific practices through in-class presentations and/or online postings with discussion.

☑ To develop critical thinking about best practices while exploring how they contribute to the overall foundation of sound budgeting.

Background

Since 1993, the GFOA has made available a wide variety of public financial management information as a public service. This material is referred to as Best Practices. The GFOA website (http://www.gfoa. org/) explains that the Best Practices are the product of broad-based development by public finance professionals. Their purpose is to support exemplary strategies and techniques for state and local government practitioners.

This online resource supports public financial management through the publication of *Best Practices* which are then posted on the GFOA's website. Upon viewing a Best Practice, you will see a title for the practice, the date when it was approve by the GFOA's Executive Board, background information, and the recommended practice. Most Best Practices include notes with references also.

Familiarity with GFOA Best Practices is a fundamental learning objective of governmental budgeting courses. The learning experience offered in this exercise challenges you to think critically about how these Best Practices contribute to sound budgeting.

Assignment

Your instructor will assign each student up to three Best Practices for review and analysis. Each student supports the class by summarizing the assigned documents from the GFOA website at http://www.gfoa.org/. Your instructor will determine whether your summary(ies) may be presented and discussed in class and/or posted and discussed online.

To view the list of documents, go to http://www.gfoa.org and click on Best Practices. The GFOA organizes these documents around broad categories as follows:

√ Accounting & Financial Reporting

√ Budgeting & Financial Planning

√ CIP/Economic Development

√ Debt Management

√ Financial Management

√ Pension & Benefits Administration

√ Technology

√ Treasury Management

Complete the GFOA's Website Best Practices Assignment Sheets. Be prepared to make a short class presentation and/or post and discuss the Best Practice online covering (1) each assigned document and (2) your critique of how each practice contributes to sound budgeting.

Name _____   Date _____

GFOA Website's Best Practices Assignment Sheets

1. Identify the first assigned Best Practice.

   Category: _____

   Title: _____

2. Summarize the major provisions of this practice.

   _____

   _____

   _____

   _____

   _____

   _____

3. How does this practice contribute to sound budgeting?

   _____

   _____

   _____

   _____

   _____

4. Identify the second assigned Best Practice.

   Category: _____

   Title: _____

5. Summarize the major provisions of this practice.

   _____

   _____

   _____

   _____

   _____

34

6. How does this practice contribute to sound budgeting?

_____

_____

_____

_____

_____

7. Identify the third assigned Best Practice.

Category: _____

Title: _____

8. Summarize the major provisions of this practice.

_____

_____

_____

_____

_____

9. How does this practice contribute to sound budgeting?

_____

_____

_____

_____

_____

Exercise 5

Revenue Forecasting

Learning Objectives:

☑   To underscore the importance of public agency revenue forecasting.

☑   To introduce the concept of "impermanent revenue" and focus on the critical reasons for treating it prudently.

☑   To familiarize you with some of the typical classes of governmental revenues while illustrating a wide range of revenue sources that call for careful scrutiny in revenue forecasts.

☑   To review the more common techniques of revenue forecasting while identifying generally accepted forecasting guidelines.

☑   To expose you to some of the real-world explanations behind revenue pattern changes.

☑   To challenge you to develop an elementary revenue forecast for an annual budget process.

Background

The Importance of Revenue Forecasting

Budget expenditure development revolves around revenue availability. Accordingly, revenue forecasts steer public agency budgeting. They project available funding and pinpoint variables that may influence revenue levels. Forecasts assist agencies to determine the sustainability of services. They also permit long-term strategic resource planning that may include capital investments.

Inaccurate forecasting can result in a variety of problems. On the one hand, overly ambitious revenue forecasts may result in program reductions or hastily considered tax and fee increases to cover for an erroneous estimate. Moreover, aggressive, risky revenue estimates at the beginning of a budget cycle may trigger larger programs that require pruning during the cycle when revenues fall short. On the other hand, underestimating revenue may give fuel to charges of excessive taxation when surpluses surface. Additionally, unexpected hardships may hit within a given budget cycle. Consequently, revenue forecasts require realistic rather than wishful thinking. That includes an analysis of whether a revenue source recurs annually or represents a one-time windfall. Sometimes, even within recurring revenues, there may be a portion of the revenue stream that has an impermanent fluctuation.

Impermanent Revenue

Impermanent revenues refer to temporary income. They occur only once or so sporadically that attempts to forecast them accurately are illusive. Consequently, the odds of forecasting impermanent revenues reliably make establishing appropriations against such revenue unproductive. Occasionally, impermanent revenues may include short-term revenue that accrues beyond a designated fiscal year.

There is no substitute for comprehensively determining the character of each revenue source in revenue forecasting. Impermanent revenues must be detected, reviewed, and sensibly appropriated. Occasionally, fiscal stability teeters on a public agency's skill in making distinctions between impermanent, one-time revenues, and recurring, ongoing revenues.

Upon determining that a revenue source is of a nonrecurring nature, analysis turns to evaluation of the most prudent use of that revenue. The objective is to garner the greatest benefit from the one-time assistance. To maintain fiscal stability, the public agency must sidestep the temptation to use impermanent revenue to fund something in one budget cycle that requires continued financial support in another cycle.

One of the greatest challenges to implementing an impermanent revenue strategy is that ongoing revenue trends are often based upon insufficient and or skewed historical data. For example, property taxes may rise 14–16% over 42 months (multiple annual budget cycles). A portion of the increase may be traceable to residential growth with considerable impact on public service delivery demands. However, the bulk of the increase above a 15-year historic trend of seven percent may be generated by new industrial developments added to the tax base. Both continue to contribute to tax proceeds. Yet it is doubtful that this atypical property tax jump will replace the long-term trend on an ongoing basis.

Faulty analysis and rosy projections lead to "boom and bust" budgets. Such patterns erode public confidence and destabilize public service planning. In the foregoing example, the more conservative course would be to give the long-term trend greater credence. The disparity between the 42-month increase and a much longer-term trend should be considered impermanent revenue. Such treatment protects the public agency from increasing ongoing expenses based on a short-term anomaly.

Typical Revenue Classes

The federal government maintains an accounting system to organize revenues into various classes for tracking, accountability, and analysis purposes. Likewise, states do the same. States also establish accounting systems and provide some procedural guidance to local governments. While there are variations between states, this exercise introduces revenue classes commonly found in California. The California State Controller's Office promulgates standards. Typical revenue classes include the following:

Taxes – compulsory charges or levies against income, property, or product use. Examples include various forms of property taxes, sales and use taxes, and transient occupancy taxes.

Licenses, Permits, and Franchises – revenues emanating from the issuance of authorizations for something. Examples include licenses for animals, businesses, occupations, and amusements as well as permits for land use, construction projects, motion pictures and franchises requiring regulation.

Fines, Forfeitures, and Penalties – revenues received as a result of offenses, legal violations, and negligence. Examples include vehicle fines, court fines, legal judgments, and penalties on delinquent taxes.

Revenue from Use of Money and Property – earnings and revenues from investments, rents, and concessions. Examples include investment income, parking fees, leases, concession payments, and various royalties.

Intergovernmental Revenues – revenues transferred from one level of government to another. Examples include highway users' tax, motor vehicle in-lieu fees, state funds for administrative and/or program delivery costs, disaster relief, public safety funds, and federal public assistance programs.

Charges for Services – revenues from costs associated with service user benefits. Examples include assessment and tax collection fees, election services, legal services, personnel services, planning and engineering services, law enforcement services, recording fees, sanitation services, and park and recreation fees.

Miscellaneous revenues – revenue not accounted for in other classes. Examples include receipts from salvage and surplus supplies, sale of various publications, tobacco settlements, insurance proceeds, and contributions from trust funds.

Other financing sources – revenue from transfers between public agencies' funds for which no reimbursement is anticipated and long-term debt proceeds.

Common Revenue Forecasting Techniques

Revenue forecasting is a technical, complex process that involves numerous variables and estimations. It blends analysis, rigorous math, and judgment. Knowledge about a public agency's revenue sources, appropriate data, and a prudent approach form the basis of revenue forecasting. At this point, we know that revenue forecasting entails calculations or predictions normally as a result of some level of study and analysis. It is data driven. Therefore, we need to consider data limitations. Data available for revenue forecasting may be inaccurate and/or incomplete. There may be too little data, or it may be too superficial to discern a pattern. Data are usually anchored in some fashion. Most commonly it is tied to time. Something happens within or over some period of time. Revenue forecasting revolves around examining data with reference to time then taking an educated stab at predicting the future. Described below are common forecasting techniques.

Projection refers to the notion that whatever happened in the past, particularly most recently, will more than likely happen again. It is a simple calculation that can be done quickly and, in some static environments, provides ballpark accuracy. However, the inevitability of changing circumstances limits the usefulness of projection. Governmental budgeting evolves, and is seldom simple.

Extrapolation relies on the extension of general trends while forecasting. One step removed from projection, it registers longer-term trends and factors those into future estimates. Extrapolation refines projections while remaining relatively quick to perform. Some trends are truly simple, and this technique efficiently predicts them. Unfortunately, much of governmental budgeting experiences sufficient variation to warrant more sophisticated techniques to improve accuracy.

Time series analysis deconstructs financial data into four components for analysis. First, long-term historical patterns are reviewed for increases and decreases. Second, periodic, or seasonal variations receive scrutiny. Third, longer-term cycles that relate to general economic conditions are taken into account. Fourth, erratic or unexplained factors can be isolated for evaluation. These pieces, once individually explored, may be reassembled to plot an overall trend. There are a number of time series based methods such as moving averages, exponential smoothing, double exponential smoothing, regression, multiple regression, and autoregressive methods. The time series analysis enriches predictability by calculating more data more closely. It does take more time and effort than projection or extrapolation.

Time series multivariant analysis refers to an upgraded version of time series analysis. It factors in more variables. Often, the time series multivariant technique earns the "econometric modeling" label when this elaboration includes a wide variety of economic factors (e.g., unemployment, job growth, construction activities, and consumer price index). A more thorough factor assessment generally produces more reliable estimates. However, greater sophistication of forecasting sometimes induces more confidence in forecasting than is warranted. Good judgment retains a place when using even the most sophisticated forecasting methods.

Delphi technique, a qualitative method, utilizes the know-how of several authorities to develop forecasting perspectives. Usually, the experts initially prepare their forecasts independently. Then, the initial forecasts are shared, reviewed, and debated in a group setting. Contributors are given the opportunity to revise their initial forecast based on what they have learned from others. The process may be repeated. The series of successive approximations tend to massage disparities toward a greater consensus. The strength of a well-managed Delphi approach rests on the richness of the collective expertise and candid questioning. On the downside, the technique takes considerable time, and paying all the experts for their work can be costly.

Common mathematical treatments support these mainstream techniques. For instance, deterministic modeling and multiple regression are used in multiple approaches. *Deterministic modeling* refers to employing a standardized formula to a revenue element or some related series of factors. It is particularly useful for own-source revenues where a jurisdiction forecasts a revenue source with a high degree of reliability. *Multiple regression* computes revenue estimates in relation to one or more independent variables.

Revenue forecasting deploys those forecasting techniques most amenable to developing high-confidence estimates. The exclusive use of one technique seldom occurs. Diverse revenue sources often call for a mix of techniques for both accuracy and efficiency.

Revenue Forecasting Guidelines

Government entities approach revenue estimation through a variety of means. The more usual guidelines are listed and explained in the following pages.

> *Analyze and project each revenue source within a revenue class independently.* This enables public agencies to consider unique revenue characteristics for each source. Each jurisdiction can review the source's legal authority, collection protocols, and receipt patterns. Most importantly, policymakers can weigh the need to make modifications. The aggregation of several, independently projected revenue sources within a revenue class provides a more accurate revenue class forecast. It mitigates forecasting errors compared with macro estimation by revenue class.

> *Focus analysis and staff resources on major components within a revenue class.* Revenue forecasting consumes staff resources. Plan and prioritize accordingly. A revenue source that generates $237 million annually needs more painstaking attention than a revenue source that brings in $10 million annually.

> *Review comparative data.* Comparative data from similar jurisdictions can be helpful sometimes. It may aid an agency to develop a greater understanding of the character of a critical revenue source. The agency initiating the comparison should assess and adjust for differences between the agencies to enhance the validity of the comparison. Such differences may include the scope and quality of services, the demographics served, and regional similarities and differences (e.g., coastal properties generally generate greater property taxes than inland regions, assuming a similar property tax rate).

Disclose assumptions. Candid and transparent description of forecasting assumptions allows others to ask informed questions and offer further refinements. It also establishes the parameters of estimates for quick reference when revisiting becomes necessary. This practice pays a twofold dividend. First, in reviewing revenue estimates, policymakers may discover areas in which to assert guidance. Second, assumption disclosure involves policymakers in overall budget accountability. This limits the opportunity for policymakers to distance themselves from sharing responsibility for missed revenue performance. Similarly, this compels them to support corrective measures when projections fall short.

Collaboration. Sound public agency revenue forecasts reflect more than candor and transparency. They are enriched with multi-directional collaboration. Internally, besides the budget staff, program directors and operational managers are often consulted. Externally, neighboring agencies may be contacted. Local governments often seek advice from their respective state government. Such collaborations take time and need to be coordinated with the requirements for timely budget adoption.

Analyze historical revenue performance data. Historical data by revenue source usually provides the most insight into future revenue performance. Generally, a reliable trend analysis requires at least five years of data. Ideally, ten years of data are desirable to increase the forecast accuracy. Beyond ten years, data may become less reliable because of changes in the fiscal environment. Constant dollar adjustments may be made to minimize distortion over time. But assumptions used should be disclosed for reference and further inquiry.

Adjust historical revenue performance conservatively. Revenue sources may have seasonal and/or cyclical components. For example, holiday winter retail sales taxes may disproportionately spike the third quarter (January–March of a July 1–June 30 fiscal year) sales tax receipts. Presidential election years skew election costs and related revenues every four years. Business cycles and emerging demographic trends may require special treatment. Additionally, atypical events such as a one-year centennial celebration with associated costs and revenues may occur sporadically. Predictable fluctuations need careful calculation. While local agencies want to be as accurate as possible, overforecasting revenue usually presents more governmental problems than underforecasting. This is the product of stakeholders demanding more and policymakers wanting to meet their demands.

Prudence, or good judgment is important. Public agencies need to be practical and minimize risk. If a revenue source's performance seems too good to be true, it probably is. Occasionally, public agencies are demonized as always "crying poverty" or are accused of being guilty of overtaxation. These claims arise when public agencies underestimate or overestimate revenues. Consequently, depending on the significance of a revenue source to overall funding, public agencies sometimes disclose high- and low-budgeted ranges of a revenue source to convey the parameters of an estimate and the volatility potential.

Now let's apply what we have learned to forecasting the revenue for Hometown City. Your forecasting should rely upon the projection, extrapolation, and time series analysis methods. Time and data limitations make the time series multivariant and Delphi methods too problematical for this exercise. However, in using the projection, extrapolation, and time series analysis methods, you need to consider the revenue forecasting guidelines summarized.

Assignment

Hometown City's Budget Director needs to develop the revenue forecast for the upcoming fiscal year. Table 1 supplies actual historical data. Additionally, it provides an estimate for the current fiscal year. Table 1 is followed by other factors that are likely to influence the upcoming fiscal year. Your task has two elements: (1) to study the data presented and (2) complete the Revenue Forecasting Assignment Sheets on pages 47–48 incorporating insights gained from Table 1 and the supporting information provided on pages 44–46. Summarize key calculations for reference and disclose any assumptions you make in developing your forecast.

Table 1 – Hometown City Revenue Forecast*

Revenue Source	2008-09 Actual	2009-10 Actual	2010-11 Actual	2011-12 Actual	2012-13 Actual	2013-14 Actual	2014-15 Actual	2015-16 Estimate	2016-17 Budget
Taxes									
Property	250,000	275,500	296,989	311,838	340,215	396,350	464,126	534,209	
Sales	219,000	229,950	243,747	253,741	266,428	282,947	294,254	306,035	
Transient occupancy	17,550	13,125	13,900	17,513	18,214	19,015	19,947	20,725	
Licenses & Permits									
Business licenses	1,171	1,203	1,226	1,253	1,503	1,530	1,560	1,590	
Building permits	2,997	3,087	3,317	3,358	3,419	3,549	3,687	3,831	
Use of Money & Property									
Parking fees	0	0	0	0	0	572	575	570	
Interest	1,170	1,386	1,490	1,319	1,460	1,570	1,769	1,730	
Concession payments	0	0	0	0	0	0	3,500	3,500	
Intergovernmental									
Motor vehicle fees	20,155	20,658	21,175	10,852	11,123	11,401	11,687	11,977	
Charges for Services									
Fire services	0	0	0	0	0	0	4,100	4,490	
Park and recreation fees	3,997	4,517	4,013	4,229	4,957	5,101	4,758	4,815	
Total	516,040	549,426	585,857	604,103	647,319	722,035	809,963	893,472	

* Figures are in the thousands of dollars (e.g., $250,000,000 is expressed as $250,000).

Supporting Information

The following information supports your revenue forecast development for 2016–17.

Taxes

√ Over the past 20 years, actual property taxes have increased by an average of 8% per year except for 2013–14, 2014–15, and the 2015–16 estimate. During 2013–14 and 2014–15, major industrial development and higher than usual housing construction were added to the tax base. The 2015–16 estimate anticipates the end of the property tax surge.

√ The state in which Hometown City is located forecasts a statewide sales tax increase of 4.7% for 2016–17. However, Hometown City historically trails the statewide sales tax proceeds' forecasts by approximately 0.5%

√ Transient occupancy taxes have averaged a modest 4.0% increase over the past 20 years with the exception of 2010–11 and 2011–12. Early in 2010–11 there was a 47,000-acre fire that took out three hotels/motels and spoiled two summer recreational seasons. The hotels/motels were rebuilt, and this revenue stream has been restored to its historical pattern.

Licenses and Permits

√ Business license fees have grown at the rate of 2.1% annually over the past 20 years. However, the City Council increased the fee by 17.5% in 2012–13 to capture the cost of personnel associated with regulating and monitoring businesses with new automation.

√ Building permit revenue fluctuates with the economy but historically averages a 3.9% increase annually. Currently, 2016–17 appears to be a typical year.

Use of Money and Property

√ Hometown City installed parking meters in 2013–14 to regulate parking in the downtown business district. Consequently, there is no long-term historical data available for analysis.

√ Historically, Hometown City experiences monthly cash flow fluctuations of many millions throughout the fiscal year. These fluctuations are based on tax collection cycles, pre-arranged concessions, fire services payments, and peak spending points (e.g., the fall/ winter acquisition of new equipment for the year and increased law enforcement during the summer tourism season). The city maintains operating capital and cash reserves that are increased about 5% annually. In 2008–09, various reserves and cash balances hovered around $30 million. These funds are invested in money market accounts and 30–90 day short-term investments to preserve liquidity for operational use while still earning some yield. Earned interest averaged 3.2% over the past 20 years. However, based on current economic conditions, interest is forecasted to grow only .3% over the 2015–16 estimate for 2016–17.

√ In 2014–15, the baseball stadium's first concession payment of $3.5 million started flowing to offset city-incurred stadium construction costs. The Hometown City Council is concerned that whereas debt service on the stadium construction is covered, unexpected city service costs beyond construction are not being reimbursed. To stem the red ink, the Council authorized the city manager to establish an events planning unit in 2014–15. The purpose of this unit is to increase stadium usage with additional gross event receipts of $12 million in 2016–17. The city anticipates concession payments of 3.0% of these gross receipts on top of the annual baseball concession fee.

Intergovernmental Revenues

√ Motor vehicle license fees have grown by an average of 2.5% over the past 20 years. In 2011–12, the state reduced the motor vehicle fee by 50% in a politically popular move.

Charges for Services

√ New City was incorporated in 2013–14 with a boundary contiguous with Hometown City. As a small but growing community, it currently contracts with Hometown City for fire protection services. The annual base contract of $4.1 million commenced in 2014–15 and has a 9.5% cost increase scheduled with each new fiscal year. Additionally, New City wants to increase fire prevention and support personnel in 2016–17. The increased revenue from this change will add another $314,000 in revenue to Hometown City in 2016–17.

√ Park and recreation fees were instituted in 2007–08 with collection starting in 2008–09. So far, city staff has not established a long-term revenue trend from this source. Data trending is problematic since there is little control over community requests that periodically bump-up revenues with special events at the more popular parks.

Name _____   Date _____

Revenue Forecasting Assignment Sheets

Provide your forecast for each revenue source listed below, then explain the reasoning behind the figures. (Express your figures in the thousands of dollars as you see in Table 1.)

1. 2016–17 Taxes

   Property: _____

   Sales: _____

   Transient occupancy: _____

   _____

   _____

   _____

   _____

   _____

   _____

2. 2016–17 Licenses & Permits

   Business licenses: _____

   Business Permits: _____

   _____

   _____

   _____

   _____

   _____

48

3. 2016–17 Use of Money & Property

Parking Fees: _____

Interest payments: _____

Concessions: _____

_____

_____

_____

_____

_____

_____

4. 2016–17 Intergovernmental Revenue

Motor vehicle fees: _____

_____

_____

5. 2016–17 Charge for Services

Fire Services: _____

Park and recreation fees: _____

_____

_____

_____

6. 2016–17 Revenue Forecast

Total: _____

Exercise 6

Program Expenditure Development

Learning Objectives:

- ☑ To immerse you in the detailed process of preparing a comprehensive budget for a small program.

- ☑ To expose you to the details of calculating personnel costs while illustrating the range of expenditures required to support a program.

- ☑ To provide examples of assumptions used in developing budgets.

- ☑ To demonstrate a range of scenarios that may be used to provide policymakers with choices regarding program funding

- ☑ To distinguish between general operational support, specialized program related expenses, and one-time start-up costs.

- ☑ To develop your fiscally-oriented critical thinking skills in sorting through cost calculation tasks.

- ☑ To challenge you to find sensible approaches to lowering the net cost of a program.

Background

Public organizations build budgets from different starting points. They assemble cost data from all personnel needs, services and supplies, equipment items, and other expenses. Often, program expenditure development rests on assumptions and estimates. This is especially true for new programs since no experience base has evolved. Expenditure-related revenues and general revenues offset costs. The budget organizes these costs in a variety of ways for specified purposes. At the foundational level, an organization may be viewed as a system of aggregated public service delivery programs with associated costs.

This exercise aids you in obtaining a feel for developing a governmental budget by focusing on a new program. It requires you to review and manipulate assumptions and data elements at the program level of analysis. The exercise uses simple math while focusing on conceptualization and fiscally oriented critical thinking. Each calculation should be rounded to the nearest dollar. You will fully develop the line item expenditures for a program proposal for initial start-up. Mimicking the real world of governmental budgeting, you must then develop alternative funding scenarios. The exercise concludes with reflective questions about the process. You will be asked to consider program-related revenue suggestions to lower the net cost of the program

Assignment

The District Attorney of University County proposes a new Sexual Predator Eradication Program for funding consideration by the Board of Supervisors (or County Commissioners). This requires program expenditure development under alternative scenarios using base salary information contained in Table 1 below and the background data that follows. Using the data in Table 1 and the background data provided below, calculate the costs for scenarios 1, 2, and 3 in the Program Expenditure Development Assignment Sheets on pages 55–60, then answer the General Questions on page 61.

Table 1 – Biweekly Salary Grade Assignments

No.*	Position Classification	Step 1	Step 2	Step 3	Step 4	Step 5
1	Chief Deputy District Attorney	5054	5306	5572	5850	6142
2	Deputy District Attorneys	3846	4039	4241	4453	4675
1	Supervising DA Investigator	3338	3506	3681	3866	4059
3	Senior DA Investigators	2983	3133	3290	3454	3627
2	DA Investigators	2641	2773	2911	3058	3210
1	Office Supervisor	2786	2926	3072	3226	3388
2	Office Assistants	2194	2303	2418	2539	2666
1	Victim Witness Advocate	2602	2732	2869	3013	3164

* The numbers in this column indicate how many employees are proposed for each classification.

Background Data

A. Salaries are calculated at 26 biweekly pay periods on a full year, fiscal year basis, with the fiscal year running from July 1 through the following June 30. For example, the salary of a Chief Deputy District Attorney at Step 1 for 26 pay periods (a full year) is calculated as follows: $5,054 × 26 pay periods = $131,404.

B. In the start-up year, salaries are computed based on the number of pay periods that the policymakers specifically approve. For example, in a fiscal year running from July 1 through June 30, a January 1 start-up date would involve funding for 13 pay periods.

C. Based on analysis of past staffing patterns, many jurisdictions find that not all positions in a new unit start at Step 1 of their respective salary range. In this assignment your calculations are to be based on the following assumptions.

- Chief Deputy District Attorney starts at Step 1 (assumes promotional opportunity).

- Deputy District Attorney positions, based on external recruiting and internal promotions, and transfers, should be budgeted at the Deputy District Attorney Step 3 level.

- The District Attorney plans to transfer a seasoned Supervising DA Investigator from within the office to fill this critical function. Assume this position qualifies for funding at Step 5.

- The Senior DA Investigator position will be filled by the internal promotion of three DA Investigators. Therefore, assume the new Senior DA investigators will start at Step 4.

- The two DA Investigators start at Step 1.

- The Office Supervisor will be transferred from within the office. Assume this position qualifies for funding at Step 5.

- The Office Assistants start at Step 1.

- The Victim Witness Advocate starts at Step 1.

D. The benefit portion of personnel costs varies tremendously based on negotiated labor contracts, occupational units, and externally determined factors such as the Social Security benefit cost rate. The following simplified range of assumptions is to be used in developing benefits associated with the staffing for the District Attorney's Sexual Predator Eradication Program.

- Assume a general retirement rate factor of 27.7% for all non-safety positions assigned to the program. This rate is applied to the salary amount. For instance, suppose the Chief Deputy District Attorney position is budgeted for a salary of $131,404 for the first year. Then, $36,399 ($131,404 × 27.7%) must be allocated for retirement costs for this position. All positions planned for the Sexual Predator Eradication Program fall under the general retirement program except the Supervising DA Investigator, Senior DA Investigators, and the DA Investigators. These positions fall under University County's safety retirement program.

- Assume a 52.9% safety retirement benefit for the aforementioned safety employees. The rate is applied to the salaries of the safety positions to determine the allocation for safety retirement.

- Social Security deductions must be collected on the standard calendar year (not fiscal year) salary amounts for each position at the rate of 6.2% up to $117,000. However, for simplicity in this exercise, assume that the Social Security rate is applied to the full fiscal year salary amounts. For example, that means that the rate of 6.2% would apply to the full salary of the Office Supervisor whose salary is below $117,000. But it would apply only to the first $117,000 fiscal year salary of the Chief Deputy District Attorney.

- A Social Security/Medicare rate of 1.45% is to be applied to all salaries to cover this benefit.

- An Unemployment Insurance rate of 0.6% is to be applied to all salary amounts to cover this benefit.

- Life Insurance coverage is to be calculated at $42 per employee per year, or $1.62 per employee bi-weekly.

- Health Insurance is to be calculated at $11,414 per employee per year, or $439 per employee bi-weekly.

- Dental Insurance is to be calculated at $624 per employee per year, or $24.00 per employee bi-weekly.

- Vision Care is to be calculated at $71 per employee per year, or $2.72 per employee bi-weekly.

E. For simplicity, no salary and benefit assumptions are included for variables that vacillate widely among public agencies including tiered retirement rates, short term disability, car allowances, differential pay for parking, uniform allowances, standby-pay, shift differentials, bilingual pay, overtime, and temporary help.

F. Services and Supplies to support this program relate to (1) general operational support for effective staffing and (2) specialized program-related expenses. Both may have start-up and ongoing components. To compile the Services and Supplies requirements, use the following simplified assumptions:

General Operational Support

- Office equipment (lower value, non-capital items such as desks, chairs, file cabinets, shelving, and credenzas) at $3,800 for each employee.

- Office expense at $200 per employee per month.

- Telephone land line service at $105 per employee per month.

- Mobile phone service at $95 per employee per month for all investigators, the Chief Deputy District Attorney, Deputy District Attorneys, and Victim Witness Advocate.

- Radios for all investigators, Chief Deputy District Attorney, and Office Supervisor at $120 per employee per month.

- Reproduction costs at $105 per employee per month.

- Casualty Insurance at $36 per month per employee.

- Workers' Compensation Insurance at $74 per employee per month for each investigator and $28 per position per month for each non-investigative employee.

- Motor pool charges for all investigators and Chief Deputy District Attorney at $535 per employee per month.

- Data processing charges $310 per employee per month.

- Initial one-time, personal computer software purchase at $695 per employee.

Specialized Operational Support

- Law enforcement sexual predator one-time database buy-in at $40,000.

- Law enforcement sexual predator database monthly access charge at $1,350 per month.

- Forensic consultants and technician services estimated at $2,500 per month.

- Miscellaneous investigative expenses as needed (e.g., informant expenses, non-forensic consultants, occasional helicopter support) estimated at $4,200 per month.

G. Equipment (i.e., items lasting more than one year and costing more than $1,000 per item, including bundled computer workstations).

- High-performance workstations for the Supervising DA Investigator and the Office Supervisor at a one-time cost of $3,100 each.

- Other staff members are furnished with a basic desktop personal computer workstation at a one-time cost of $1,950 each.

- One high-speed color printer at a one-time cost of $2,400.

Name _____   Date _____

Program Expenditure Development Assignment Sheets
Scenario 1:

1. Develop the budget requirements for a 12-month operation (26 pay periods) of the District Attorney's proposed Sexual Predator Eradication Program using the given budget development assumptions and data elements. Display the results of your calculations in the table below. It structures the data while providing an example using the Chief Deputy District Attorney position classification.

Scenario 1: Salary and Benefits Table

Position Class.*	Salary	Retire.	SS	Med.	UI	LI	HI	Dent.	Vis.	Total
1 Chief Dep. DA	131404	36399	7254	1905	788	42	11414	624	71	189901
2 Dep. DA										
1 Sup. DA Inves.										
3 Sr. DA Inves.										
2 DA Inves.										
1 Office Sup.										
2 Office Asst.										
1 VW Adv.										
Grand Totals										

* Under the Position Class. (Position Classification) column, the number of employees proposed for each classification is given first. When calculating the total costs, remember to take this into consideration. For example, the salary cost for two Deputy District Attorneys for 26 pay periods, at Step 3 equals $220,532).

Listed below is a key to the abbreviations used in the Salary and Benefits Table.

Chief Dep. DA – Chief Deputy District Attorney   Retire. – Retirement

Dep. DA – Deputy District Attorney   SS – Social Security

Sup. DA Inves. – Supervising DA Investigator   Med. – Social Security – Medicare

Sr. DA Inves. – Senior DA Investigator   UI – Unemployment Insurance

DA Inves – DA Investigator   LI – Life Insurance

Office Sup. – Office Supervisor   HI – Health Insurance

Office Asst. – Office Assistant   Dent. – Dental Insurance

VW Adv. – Victim Witness Advocate   Vis. – Vision Care

Services and Supplies

Office Equipment   _____

Office Expenses   _____

Telephone Land Line Charges   _____

Mobile Phone Charges   _____

Radio Charges   _____

Reproduction Charges   _____

Casualty Insurance   _____

Workers' Comp. Insurance   _____

Motor Pool Charges   _____

Data Processing Charges   _____

Software Purchases   _____

One-time Database Buy-in   _____

Monthly Database Charge   _____

Forensic Services   _____

Misc. Investigative Expenses   _____

Total Services and Supplies   _____

Equipment

High-performance Computer
Workstation   _____

Computer Workstations   _____

High Speed Color Printer   _____

Total Equipment   _____

Total 12-Month Program Budget

Salary and Benefit   _____

Services and Supplies   _____

Equipment   _____

Total   _____

2. Identify all one-time costs associated with the program start-up:

_____

_____

_____

_____

_____

_____

Scenario 2:

3. Assume the elected policymakers decide to fund the District Attorney's proposed Sexual Predator Eradication Program. However, the majority decide that the program cannot be funded until February, or seven months into the fiscal year. Develop the budget requirements for the remaining five months. Assume funding is required for 11 pay periods. Display the results of your calculations in the table below. It structures the data while providing an example using the Chief Deputy District Attorney position classification.

Scenario 2: Salary and Benefits Table

(For a key to the abbreviations see page 55)

Position Class.*	Salary	Retire.	SS	Med.	UI	LI	HI	Dent.	Vis.	Total
1 Chief Dep. DA	55594	15400	3447	806	334	18	4829	264	30	80722
2 Dep. DA										
1 Sup. DA Inves.										
3 Sr. DA Inves.										
2 DA Inves.										
1 Office Sup.										
2 Office Asst.										
1 VW Adv.										
Grand Totals										

* Under the Position Class. (Position Classification) column, the number of employees proposed for each classification is given first. When calculating the total costs, remember to take this into consideration.

58

Services and Supplies

Office Equipment
_____

Office Expenses
_____

Telephone Land Line Charges
_____

Mobile Phone Charges
_____

Radio Charges
_____

Reproduction Charges
_____

Casualty Insurance
_____

Workers' Comp. Insurance
_____

Motor Pool Charges
_____

Data Processing Charges
_____

Software Purchases
_____

One-time Database Buy-in
_____

Monthly Database Charge
_____

Forensic Services
_____

Misc. Investigative Expenses
_____

Total Services and Supplies
_____

Equipment

High-performance Computer Workstation
_____

Computer Workstations
_____

High Speed Color Printer
_____

Total Equipment
_____

Total 11 Pay Periods Program Budget

Salary and Benefit
_____

Services and Supplies
_____

Equipment
_____

Total
_____

Scenario 3:

4. Using the budget requirements developed in Scenario 1, the elected policy-makers have decided to fund the program requested by the District Attorney but at a reduced level and with a January 1 start-up date. Delete one Deputy District Attorney, two Senior DA Investigators, one DA Investigator, and one Office Assistant. Assume the reduced program is operational for 13 pay periods. Display the results of your calculations in the table below. It structures the data while providing an example using the Chief Deputy District Attorney position classification.

Scenario 3: Salary and Benefits Table

(For a key to the abbreviations see page 55)

Position Class.*	Salary	Retire.	SS	Med.	UI	LI	HI	Dent.	Vis.	Total
1 Chief Dep. DA	65702	18199	4074	953	394	21	5707	312	35	95397
1 Dep. DA										
1 Sup. DA Inves.										
1 Sr. DA Inves.										
1 DA Inves.										
1 Office Sup.										
1 Office Asst.										
1 VW Adv.										
Grand Totals										

* Under the Position Class. (Position Classification) column, the number of employees proposed for each classification is given first. When calculating the total costs, remember to take this into consideration.

60

Services and Supplies

Office Equipment _____

Office Expenses _____

Telephone Land Line Charges _____

Mobile Phone Charges _____

Radio Charges _____

Reproduction Charges _____

Casualty Insurance _____

Workers' Comp. Insurance _____

Motor Pool Charges _____

Data Processing Charges _____

Software Purchases _____

One-time Database Buy-in _____

Monthly Database Charge _____

Forensic Services _____

Misc. Investigative Expenses _____

Total Services and Supplies _____

Equipment

High-performance Computer Workstation _____

Computer Workstations _____

High Speed Color Printer _____

Total Equipment _____

Total 13 Pay Periods, Reduced Program Budget

Salary and Benefit _____

Services and Supplies _____

Equipment _____

Total _____

Exercise 6 Program Expenditure Development

General Questions:

5. What cost calculations did you find the most troublesome and why?

_____

_____

_____

_____

_____

_____

6. This exercise represents a simplified approach to developing budget requirements for a small program. Identify and explain three other cost components that could be interjected into the development of a real-world budget for this program.

_____

_____

_____

_____

_____

7. Suppose you are tasked with generating revenue to offset the cost of this program. Identify and explain three sources you would suggest for exploration.

_____

_____

_____

_____

_____

_____

_____

Exercise 7

Budgeting Equipment

Learning Objectives:

☑ To familiarize you with equipment justification, analysis, and budgeting.

☑ To enable you to distinguish between different classes of equipment.

☑ To engage you in devising approaches to review and prioritize equipment purchase decisions.

☑ To develop critical thinking skills by applying what you have learned about budgeting equipment to a challenging proposal.

Background

Effective program planning requires that public agency staff acquire equipment needed to support the accomplishment of desired performance outcomes. In this exercise, we examine four classes of equipment: direct position-linked, indirect position-linked, replacement, and new. This assignment concludes with you analyzing a proposal involving a costly equipment request with staffing, operational, and service performance issues.

Equipment Defined

Employees frequently need certain equipment to carry out assigned duties. These are items beyond those considered service and supply costs (e.g., tablets, folders, and staplers). Equipment items serve as a subset of capital assets. Capital assets represent tangible property acquired by a jurisdiction. They retain monetary value and last longer than an annual budget cycle. Whereas statutory language may define equipment, jurisdictions often have some leeway in specifying what is categorized as equipment by specifying a threshold dollar value at purchase such as

"$1,000 or more" or "$4,000 or more." For instance, a local government may determine that equipment in its jurisdiction costing more than $4,000 and with utility beyond one year, will be defined as tangible property. Once parameters are set, equipment purchases require specialized accounting treatment that involves maintaining inventories and accountability for equipment disposal. The term *fixed assets* is used synonymously with capital assets. While equipment falls within the capital assets accounting classification, land, buildings and improvements, and infrastructure such as roads, bridges, sewer systems, dams or sidewalk can also be included.

Direct Position-Linked Equipment

The need for certain equipment is directly linked to staff positions. These may be referred to as *direct position-linked* equipment. Those involved in budget development require sufficient information to determine if a particular equipment is position-linked. For instance, each park worker may require a truck. However, for every three park workers, only one $9,000 field lawn mower is required. Hence, while the trucks are position-linked equipment, the field lawn mower is not. A standard practice in law enforcement further illustrates this point. Often, an allocation of five patrol staff may represent one 24-hours/7-days-a-week patrol unit in a geographic region. Usually, policymakers and staff unhesitatingly see the service change cost of one additional, fully equipped patrol vehicle as axiomatic with the five patrol staff. Without it, the jurisdiction will not be able to provide a 24/7 patrol unit presence in the designated geographic area.

Sometimes, position-linked fixed asset needs are not readily apparent and require an in-depth analysis. For example, to respond to the earlier issue, patrol cars do not operate uninterruptedly 24/7. They require repair and maintenance and even body work after a collision. Additionally, patrol shift patterns and law enforcement needs may require overlapping vehicle usage that cannot be accommodated with only one patrol vehicle per allocation of five patrol staff. The public agency must then determine the number of vehicles that are required beyond the base vehicle to ensure that vehicles are available for shift overlaps as well as maintenance. Suppose a jurisdiction has 100 patrol staff, covering 20 24/7 patrol beats in a geographic region. How many patrol vehicles are required to ensure 24/7 fielding of patrol staff? Analysis may find that for every 24/7 patrol unit planned, 1.3 vehicles are needed. Anything less means patrol staff are doubling-up in cars or are not deployed at all. Consequently, the public agency needs to provide 26 vehicles to ensure proper deployment of 100 patrol staff. As you can see, this becomes crucial analytical information for the budgeting of patrol staff and fielding of the planned service delivery. Consequently, an accurate equipment allocation assessment needs to be maintained or else service expectations will not be met.

Equipment items often have related costs required to make them fully functional as intended. Continuing with the patrol vehicle example, patrol vehicles purchased on a volume discount basis may cost $28,000 each. However, they are not duty operational at purchase. Several features normally are added after purchase. These items, depending upon the jurisdiction's definition of equipment, may be budgeted under services and supplies. They might include a cage separator between front and rear seat, light bar and siren, radio, shotgun, laptop computer, and even a distinctive paint job with the agency's name and motto. This may increase the base patrol vehicle cost from $28,000 to several thousand more. Once again, analysis has determined that these costs must be added as part of the allocation required to make the base patrol vehicle ready to roll.

Indirect Position-Linked Equipment

Occasionally, governmental operations require *indirect position-linked* equipment. Indirect position-linked equipment items arise more from strategic issues and may be only remotely related to staffing subtleties. Again, consider the hypothetical case of 100 patrol staff, covering 20 24/7 patrol beats in a geographic area. Analysis reveals that every day, each patrol unit consumes an average of 30 minutes traveling to and from the geographic patrol area to the public agency's fuel farm. This represents an annual loss of 3,650 patrol hours (20 patrol units × 30 minutes of traveling for fuel per day × 365 days annually = 219,000 lost patrol minutes ÷ 60 minutes per hour = 3,650 hours of patrol time). Operational evaluation reveals that this time may be recaptured and redeployed to patrol duties with the indirect, position-linked installation of a centrally located fueling pump in the patrol region for $82,000. Consequently, while this represents added cost, installing a centrally located fueling pump provides more than commensurate, offsetting benefits over the foreseeable long-term.

General Review of Equipment

Budget requests may include both replacement and new, never before considered, equipment. In comparison to more costly staffing elements of most public agency budgets, equipment items represent more of a justification/defensibility issue rather than a major cost issue. During a budget squeeze or in recessionary times, public agencies often temporarily forgo replacement and new equipment to avoid staff reductions and accompanying service cutbacks. What to include in a budget calls for good judgement. Prudent decisions arise through painstaking analysis of equipment needs.

Replacement Equipment

Replacement equipment requests signify previously justified, budgeted, and acquired items. Presumably, the equipment continues to be necessary but is no longer operable or has outlived its relative utility. What are the analytical questions that require answers before policymakers determine that replacement is justifiable and approve budget funding? Although some items may require more individual investigation, some conventional questions to ask when considering replacing equipment are:

√ What is the condition of the equipment to be replaced? Does it really need to be replaced?

√ Would it be more cost effective, providing more relative value with acceptable performance, to repair rather than replace the item?

√ What performance advantages could accrue as a result of replacement? Does the new equipment offer greater benefits relative to costs?

√ What service performance and length of service were received from the existing equipment? What is the expected service performance and service length projected for the replacement equipment?

√ What is the downside to equipment replacement?

√ In replacing common items among departments, are there standards that would ensure volume cost breaks and/or extended warranties? Are standards necessary to guarantee that public agency staff can perform maintenance and support functions. For example, should a standard bundled computer workstation be developed to facilitate staff support?

New Equipment

New equipment items require even more justification and careful review than do replacement items. After all, once a public agency adds an equipment item to the inventory, organizations tend to deal merely with replacement rather than revisit the original justification. Typical questions revolve around the service case for acquisition, relative cost, and operational impacts such as:

√ How are tasks currently performed without the new item?

√ Why is the equipment needed? What contribution will it make to service delivery?

√ What is its cost? Are there ways to reduce or manage the cost over time through, for example, volume discounts or lease-purchase?

√ What are the results of comparative analysis of similar products?

√ What is required to exploit the advantages of the new equipment

√ What operational costs will decrease or increase as a result of the acquisition of the equipment?

√ What warranties or cost effective service/maintenance agreements are available?

√ What is the priority of the equipment among other equipment items and other budgetary requests overall?

Equipment Priority

Establishing equipment priority becomes necessary due to competitive jockeying for resources within organizational subunits. There is no universal criterion for equipment priorities. Often, priorities are situational and may vary widely among public agencies. Common motivations for giving priority to one equipment item over another include the following:

√ To comply with legal requirements or policy changes.

√ To ensure employee and public safety.

√ To support staffing changes to maximize service delivery outcomes

√ To save resources either immediately or over time.

√ To improve service levels through greater efficiency, economy, and effectiveness.

√ To provide reliability and sometimes provide for risk management redundancy.

Assignment

University County currently deploys 100 patrol staff to cover 20, 24/7 patrol units for the service region known as South County–Beat 1. The new sheriff continues to campaign for progressive law enforcement and maximizing the use of contemporary technology to fight crime. He proposes adding a Helicopter Support Unit to Beat 1 to (1) increase proactive patrol surveillance, (2) enhance suspect apprehension support, and (3) improve rapid deployment of tactical personnel to critical situations. Please detail your budget review questions regarding the Sheriff's proposal based on your governmental budgeting learning to date and your familiarity with equipment analysis. Organize your questions on the Budget Equipment Assignment Sheets.

Name _____   Date _____

Budgeting Equipment Assignment Sheets

1. **Proposal justification** – What questions do you have regarding the rationale for the Helicopter Support Unit?

   _____

   _____

   _____

   _____

   _____

   _____

   _____

   _____

2. **Performance information** – What projected outcome information would be helpful to review? What performance data should be maintained to evaluate long-term cost effectiveness?

   _____

   _____

   _____

   _____

   _____

   _____

   _____

   _____

3. **Operational issues** – How will the operation of the Helicopter Support Unit alter the existing patrol services in South County–Beat 1?

_____

_____

_____

_____

_____

4. **Staffing** – What staffing issues accompany the Helicopter Support Unit?

_____

_____

_____

_____

_____

5. **Services and supplies implications** – What allocations are required to support the Helicopter Support Unit?

_____

_____

_____

_____

_____

6. **Equipment information** – What equipment cost questions do you have relating to issues such as acquisition costs, operational costs, and insurance?

_____

_____

_____

_____

_____

_____

_____

_____

7. **Programmatic options** – What programmatic alternatives could you suggest to decrease the cost of the proposed capability?

_____

_____

_____

_____

_____

_____

_____

_____

Exercise 8

Exploring Public Financial Management Websites

Learning Objectives:

☑ To acquaint you with the wide variety of websites available through the Internet to support your success with public financial management.

☑ To familiarize you with specific financial management websites through online research, class presentations, and discussion.

☑ To develop critical thinking about Internet resources and consider how they may contribute to advancing sound budgeting.

Background

There are many websites that can support improved governmental budgeting and public financial management. Familiarity with nationally-oriented websites may provide critical resources to assist your agency and support your professional performance. Similarly, state websites also provide some supportive resources, albeit with considerable variation. Access to your state website to check its web page offerings usually can be accomplished by entering the name of the state followed by the term "official website." For example, entering "New Jersey official website" leads you to the homepage of the State of New Jersey. Once there, you may use the website's "search feature(s)" or "site map" to navigate to particular web pages of interest.

The architecture of state websites is not standardized. This makes comparisons among states difficult. Additionally, variances in institutional structures among states compound the difficulty of providing guidance on exploring state-based financial management web pages. Two forms of assistance are offered to aid you in finding relevant web pages for your state. First, examples of websites providing helpful public financial management information for the State of California are listed for reference. Similar web pages may be found within other state websites. Second, a survey of 26 of the 50 state websites reveals the relative availability of certain fiscally oriented web pages. Only those search terms resulting in a 50% or higher "hit" rate among the surveyed states are listed for assistance.

Listed below are examples of websites that offer some supportive resources on public financial management. (Several require registration to access key documents and reports.)

Federal Agencies Websites

United States (U.S.) Government Official Web Portal
http://www.usa.gov/

U.S. Bureau of the Census
http://www.census.gov/

U.S. Congressional Budget Office
http://www.cbo.gov/

U.S. Department of Labor, Bureau of Labor Statistics
http://www.bls.gov/

U.S. Department of the Treasury
http://www.ustreas.gov/

U.S. General Accountability Office
http://www.gao.gov/

U.S. Office of Management and Budget
http://www.whitehouse.gov/omb/

Non-Government Nationally Oriented Websites

American Association for Budget and Program Analysis
http://www.aabpa.org

American Institute of Certified Public Accountants
http://www.aicpa.org/

Brookings/Urban Institute Tax Policy Center
http://taxpolicycenter.org/index.cfm

Center for State and Local Government Excellence
http://www.slge.org

Center on Budget and Policy Priorities
http://www.cbpp.org/

Chartered Institute of Public Finance and Accountancy
http://www.cipfa.org.uk/

Fitch Ratings
https://www.fitchratings.com/web/en/dynamic/fitch-home.jsp

Governmental Accounting Standards Board
  http://www.gasb.org/main.html

Howard Jarvis Taxpayers Association
  http://www.hjta.org/

IBM Center for the Business of Government
  http://www.businessofgovernment.org

ING Institute for Retirement Research
  http://www.ingretirementresearch.com

Institute for Internal Auditors
  http://www.theiia.org/

International City/County Management Association
  http://www.icma.org

International Public Sector Accounting Standards Board
  http://www.ifac.org/PublicSector

Moody's Investors Service
  http://www.moodys.com/cust/default.asp

National Association of Counties
  http://www.naco.org/

National Association of State Budget Officers
  http://www.nasbo.org/

National League of Cities
  http://www.nlc.org/

National Taxpayers Union & National Taxpayers Union Foundation
  http://www.ntu.org/main/

Nelson A. Rockefeller Institute of Government
  http://www.rockinst.org

PEW Charitable Trusts
  http://www.pewtrusts.org

Public Entity Risk Institute
  http://www.riskinstitute.org

Public Technology Institute
  http://www.pti.org

Standard & Poor's
  http://www.standardandpoors.com/

Tax Foundation
  http://taxfoundation.org/

Urban Institute
  http://www.urban.org/index.cfm

U.S. Chamber of Commerce
  http://www.uschamber.com/

California State Government Websites

State of California Official Web Portal
http://www.ca.gov/

California Debt and Investment Advisory Commission
http://www.treasurer.ca.gov/cdiac/

California Department of Finance
http://www.dof.ca.gov/

California Legislative Analyst Office
http://www.lao.ca.gov/laoapp/main.aspx

California State Controller's Office
http://www.sco.ca.gov/

California State Treasurer
http://www.treasurer.ca.gov/

Financial Information System for California
http://www.fiscal.ca.gov/

Non-California State Oriented Websites

California Chamber of Commerce
http://www.calchamber.com/

California League of Cities
http://www.cacities.org/

California State Association of Counties
http://www.csac.counties.org/

California Tax Payers' Association
http://www.caltax.org/index.html

State Website Search Terms Survey

A survey of the 50 US states found that each of their respective official government websites provides a copy of the annual budget that can be downloaded. Furthermore, 26 of the 50 state websites reveals the relative frequency of reaching a state-based web page useful to budgeting and financial management. Search terms/topics and their relative "hit" rate follow. Only search terms/topics with a hit rate of 50% or higher among surveyed states are listed. You will likely discover that a web search of several of the terms/topics lead you to the same state website, albeit to different pages or sections of that website.

Search Term	Frequency
Auditor of Public Accounts Legislative Auditing State Auditor State Audits Division	89%
State Treasurer Treasury	87%
Department of Administration Department of Finance Department of Finance & Administration Division or Department of Planning & Budget Division of Financial Management Executive Office for Administration & Finance Office of Budget Office of Management & Budget Office of Policy & Management Office of State Finance State Budget & Management Division	76%
Accounting Office State Controller or Comptroller	53%
Department of Revenue	50%

Assignment

Your instructor will assign each student up to two public financial management websites for review and analysis. Since many of the government websites are quite extensive, your instructor might assign two or more students to research different topics on the same website. Each student supports the class by summarizing the assigned financial management website. Student summaries may be presented and discussed in class to expose you to web-based resources.

Complete the Exploring Public Financial Management Website Assignment Sheets on pages 79–80. Be prepared to make a class presentation that covers each website's purpose and contents. Then explain how the website could be useful to governmental budgeting and/or public financial management.

Name _____   Date _____

Exploring Public Financial Management Websites
Assignment Sheets

Website Name   _____

URL   _____

1. What is the purpose of the website?

   _____

   _____

   _____

   _____

2. What content is available from the website?

   _____

   _____

   _____

   _____

   _____

   _____

   _____

   _____

   _____

3. How could this website be useful to governmental budgeting and/or public
   financial management?

   _____

   _____

   _____

   _____

   _____

   _____

80

Website Name   _____

URL   _____

    1. What is the purpose of the website?

    _____

    _____

    _____

    _____

    2. What content is available from the website?

    _____

    _____

    _____

    _____

    _____

    _____

    _____

    _____

    3. How could this website be useful to governmental budgeting and/or public financial management?

    _____

    _____

    _____

    _____

    _____

    _____

    _____

Exercise 9

Capital Budgeting

Learning Objectives:

√ To define capital budgeting and related terms.

√ To familiarize you with the variety and characteristics of capital improvements in governmental budgeting.

√ To review the typical phases of developing a capital budget.

√ To challenge you to devise approaches for reviewing capital improvement needs and for determining which capital items to budget.

Background

Capital budgeting refers to a process that begins with assessment and results in provisions for maintaining expensive assets that retain usefulness over an extended period of time. It provides for the acquisition of land, buildings, and various kinds of infrastructure (e.g., roads, runways, sewer lines, and water treatment plants). These capital assets are essential to public service delivery and are supportive of community and economic development. Capital budgeting focuses on aligning prioritized projects with price tags to time schedules with funding mechanisms. This entails multiyear planning, expenditure and revenue forecasting, and financing.

Operational program planning runs parallel to capital budgeting implementation. It involves the integration of a capital asset into ongoing governmental business. For example, a new hospital usually brings more space, improved functional design, and cutting-edge technology. Activation of the hospital may also require more janitorial and security staff, upgrading staff training or new technical support positions, increased utility costs, modifications to standard operating procedures, and increased insurance coverage.

Terms related to capital budgeting include capital budget, capital expenditure, capital financing, capital improvement program, and capital needs assessment. *Capital budget* (also called capital improvement budget) refers to a separate document, or a separate section of an overall operating budget that appropriates funds for capital assets. *Capital expenditure* represents a legally authorized cost related to the provision of a capital asset. *Capital financing* provides the funding means to build or to purchase a capital asset. This may occur through annual budgeting, pay-as-you-go financing, or any number of other means used to raise funds to offset capital asset costs. *Capital improvement program* (CIP) identifies a long-term plan, usually three to seven years, with prioritized projects, expected costs, identified financing strategies, and critical timelines. *Capital needs assessment* forecasts anticipated facilities and infrastructure needs for the foreseeable long-term and precedes CIP development. Often such planning evolves out of larger strategic planning processes that governmental entities may entertain periodically.

Capital Budgeting Characteristics

Capital budgeting has several distinct characteristics. Beyond the relative expensiveness and elongated life cycle of capital assets, capital budgeting affects financial planning over multiple funding cycles. Established capital assets may require maintenance and spark replacement debates as they depreciate and become obsolete. Bringing a capital asset online may require substantial organizational effort over an extended planning horizon. Many capital assets provoke such urgent demand and enormous costs that they necessitate debt financing. Such financing, as well as operational start-up and periodic maintenance, may demand varied levels of funds from year to year.

One of the more common types of governmental capital assets involves building construction. Depending on complexity and magnitude, the completion time for the construction of a building often spans more than one fiscal year. Funds for a project still in progress at the end of the fiscal year are encumbered and carried forward to complete the work. Project phases usually include scope development and planning, design and engineering, solicitation and award of bids, construction, and project acceptance.

General Capital Budgeting Strategy

Many governmental agencies approach capital budgeting similarly. However, variations in budgetary strategy among jurisdictions exist, reflecting organizational nuances, comparative community resources, and sometimes the relative age of the area an agency serves. Usually, capital budgeting begins with policymakers or the administrative leadership initiating an evaluation of existing facilities and infrastructure. Typically, an assessment of immediate and long-term needs supplements the evaluation of current capital assets.

After compiling the capital asset needs, the budgeting staff outlines the parameters of proposals and develops a preliminary cost estimate. The estimates must reflect costs as comprehensively as possible and anticipate inflationary cost pressures over time. These could include land acquisition, environmental studies, architecture and engineering fees, construction, change order contingencies, and furnishings. Capital asset costing compels sensitivity to and coordination with operational cost impacts. For instance, it does little good to complete a jail expansion if staffing and operational expenses have not been addressed. The jurisdiction could end up with a new facility that it cannot staff or financially support.

With preliminary cost estimates in hand, the public agency reviews the range of options available to fund each asset. Funding options may consist of a one-time appropriation, yearly reserve additions until all or a portion of the asset is funded, or debt financing mechanisms. Each approach must consider short- and long-term expenditure and revenue forecasts, the use of impermanent funds, operational cash flows, other governmental assistance (such as state grants and federal earmarks), relative affordability, legal obligations, and stakeholder interests. If some means of debt financing is entertained, then costs associated with the following must also be computed.

√ Debt interest on funds borrowed √ Bond counsel

√ Disclosure counsel √ Financial advisor

√ Trustee/pay agent √ Official statement printing

√ Rating agency √ Underwriter discount or premium

√ Insurance premiums √ Credit enhancements

Once projects are identified, delivery time projected, costs estimated, and financing planned, policymakers and jurisdictional stakeholders must come to grips with relative capital asset priorities.

Prioritizing Capital Assets

Public agencies rarely meet all of their capital asset needs readily. Determining the priority of each planned capital asset is often problematic. Furthermore, every public agency prioritizes capital assets differently. A relatively small jurisdiction with little to invest may have no problem determining that building a fire station in a new development should be the clear priority. In contrast, a populous, urban area with a depressed economy and limited funds may have scores of aging structures requiring costly maintenance or replacement. In such circumstances, public agencies generally use some system of comparative analysis to rank capital projects. Some variation or combination of four strategies generally form the basis for prioritizing capital projects: executive assessment, project criticality, weighted ranking, and elected policymaker direction.

Executive assessment represents the leading method for public agencies to rank capital projects. In this approach, senior managers within a public agency recommend priorities to elected policymakers. Managers take into account costs, benefits, funding sources, as well as a sense of the community's preferences. However, this approach has several drawbacks. First, the volume and diversity of projects makes it difficult for executive assessment to consider accurately all facets of all projects. Second, project complexity often requires extra assessment time and special expertise not readily available. Third, projects generate supporters and detractors. Sifting through stakeholder perspectives sometimes bogs down the decision timeline and smothers assessment with an overwhelming amount of information.

Project criticality evaluations prioritize capital projects based on importance. Projects may be given priority for a number of reasons, including legal or regulatory requirements, health and safety concerns, elected policymaker guidance, risk management issues, or public service interests. Those projects receiving positive evaluation on more than one factor usually rank higher.

The number, variety, and complexity of capital projects may necessitate a formal *weighted ranking*. Weighted rankings are typically numbers assigned to projects based on quantitative and/or qualitative evaluations used for comparisons. For instance, on a scale from 1 to 5, 5 being the highest, a project meeting a pressing legal requirement may be weighted as a "5." A project that has only some neighborhood public support as a community enhancement may be weighted only as a "1." Typically, legal and regulatory mandates as well as health and safety issues receive the highest weights.

In the *elected policymaker direction* method, general functional guidelines such as public safety over parks and recreation are often used. Additionally, elected officials may establish preferences among rather equally weighted projects. These preferences are often politically motivated. For example, a city council's highest regular priority may be public safety. But when two councilmen run for reelection they may rank the new park and library in the city's fastest growing area with many new voters higher than they rank the expansion of the overcrowded police department's building.

As with general governmental budgeting, appropriating funds for one capital asset may mean some other needed item drops off the CIP list or finds its value compromised through deferral. Some deferrals may still consume resources for maintenance or inefficiencies even though the larger cost of addressing the item slides forward. Deferred projects sometime face fierce inflationary and scope creep pressures. (Whereas the scope of projects may grow or recede, project proponents tend to make increasingly more elaborate modifications in their plans as they contemplate acquisition of the capital asset. Scope creep refers to this tendency to make project changes that were not in the original plan.)

Assignment

In this exercise you will have the opportunity to recommend capital budget priorities for a municipality called Highpoint City. Historically, Highpoint City devotes approximately 15% of its annual budget to its capital improvement program. One-third of this amount, or 5% of the annual Highpoint budget, funds maintenance, repair, and remodeling projects. The other 10% funds new projects. In this exercise, you are not concerned with the cost, scope, or funding mechanisms for each project. As an administrative analyst on the city manager's staff, you are tasked with the responsibility for reviewing available information, recommending priorities, and explaining your rationale for (1) maintenance, repair, and remodeling projects, and (2) new capital assets. The city manager will review your proposed priority and rationale with the city council.

Part I: Maintenance, Repair, and Remodeling Projects

The following maintenance, repair, and remodeling projects are under review. Rank these priorities from highest to lowest and explain your rationale for the recommended rankings on Part I of the Capital Budgeting Assignment Sheets on pages 89–90.

Downtown Re-roofing Projects: Three 15–18-year-old downtown city public service buildings need immediate roof replacement. Previously, funds were budgeted to complete these re-roofing projects in the current year's budget. However, the city council cancelled the projects and shifted the funds to address emergency service needs associated with a fire that took out 87 homes and damaged much of Greenly Park. This past winter, rainfall was above normal. One of the buildings originally scheduled for re-roofing suffered major water damage on the top two floors. No one was injured. Yet, several computers valued at $137,000 were lost because of the leaky roof. The city may be just a storm away from further damage and/or public and staff injuries caused by roof leaks.

Police Holding Cells Retrofit: The city operates an old, six-bed holding facility used for temporary prisoner custody prior to transporting detainees to the county jail. Last year, a detainee committed suicide by hanging herself from an exposed plumbing pipe jutting out from the ceiling in the corner of her cell. The detainee's family has filed a $5 million lawsuit against the city. Since the suicide, the State Board of Corrections has conducted an inspection and found the city's holding cells to be in violation of safety standards. The police holding cell retrofit will bring the facility into compliance with state regulations.

City Hall Refurbishing: The new mayor was elected, in part, on a campaign of improving government responsiveness through his "Citizens First Campaign" devoted to better customer service. Symbolic of that emphasis, the mayor has pushed for extensive refurbishing of City Hall. The project includes interior and exterior paint, carpeting, new public lobby furniture, state-of-the-art technology upgrades in the council chambers, as well as new auditorium seating in the chambers.

Repaint and Re-carpet General Services Building: Although 21 years old, the General Services Building still meets its critical mission of providing housing for several city staff functions. Yet, because it receives few members of the public, maintenance has repeatedly been deferred. The interior and exterior desperately need paint. The original worn, tattered, and stained carpet requires replacement. The employees' union has started filing grievances over the building's general unsightly appearance. Grievances filed over the condition of the carpet have captured the attention of the State Occupational Safety and Health Administration which has issued one previous report that embarrassed the city and provoked a negative newspaper editorial.

City Hall Heating and Air Conditioning Replacement: The city's 23-year-old heating and air conditioning system is overdue for replacement. The city has deferred this project the past five years because of other priorities. The system required $92,000 in emergency repairs last summer. Despite this investment, the system could break down anytime. Staff determined that a replacement system would be more cost efficient, resulting in a significant savings in electricity use over the long run. Additionally, coinciding with the upcoming fiscal year, the electrical service provider is offering to underwrite 25% of the replacement cost for public agencies if their new systems also include a solar power component. Staff estimate that with the replacement incentives for the solar components, replacing the system will pay for itself in 10 years while reducing energy consumption by 18% on an ongoing basis.

Patching and Slurry-sealing 75 Miles of City Streets: Highpoint's public works director was quoted as saying, "pay me now, or pay me later." And, "if you chose to pay later, you will pay much more." Unmaintained roads deteriorate much faster than maintained roads. Rapid deterioration results in geometrically increased costs since more road base reconstruction must be funded to return poor streets to acceptable and maintainable use. Highpoint City has a need to patch and slurry-seal 90–100 miles of city streets annually for optimum cost effectiveness and street longevity. Five years ago the city council adopted a policy of funding only 75 miles of maintenance annually due to several community challenges and constrained resources in recent years. This policy was enacted to protect existing roads as much as possible while awaiting new revenue streams from the operation of a major shopping center when it is completed in two years. Once the shopping center revenues stabilize, the city council says it will revise the policy to fund 110 miles of city street maintenance annually.

Part II: New Capital Assets

The following new capital assets are under review. Rank these priorities from highest to lowest, and explain your rationale for the recommended rankings on Part II of the Capital Budgeting Assignment Sheets on pages 90–91.

City Fuel Farm: Currently, Highpoint City uses a central gas station for gasoline and diesel fuel for its fleet. The city re-bids the contract every five years to ensure competitive pricing. Staff research indicates that if the city invests in the construction and operation of its own fuel farm, the return on investment offsets construction costs within three years. Beyond recouping initial construction costs, ongoing fuel costs will be reduced by 21% during the fourth year and thereafter. The fueling contract will go out to bid in three years. Site acquisition and construction is projected to take just under two years.

Greenly Park: Greenly Park, the most visited park on the city's southern border, was closed to the public last year due to a fire in a neighboring canyon. The fire burned over seven acres of the 11-acre park. Besides trees, shrubbery, and grass, all tot-lot equipment, a men's restroom, and the community recreation building were destroyed. Area residents clamor for immediate re-landscaping and restoration of the tot-lot and the facilities lost. The Greenly Park Neighborhood Association faithfully sends three members to request funds for restoration and re-opening of the park during the public comment portion of every city council meeting. The council representative for the area agrees with the Association and constantly pushes for priority treatment.

Regional Youth Soccer Complex: Based on demographic analysis and community surveys, substantial interest exists in Highpoint City for a regional youth soccer complex. The initial cash outlay for land and construction represents a formidable hurdle for such a facility. The state offers a 50/50 match grant from State Parks and Recreation Bond funds and has advised the city that the project is likely to receive funding if the city commits to the match. Once established, city staff propose to implement a strategy involving advertising and concessionaire revenues projected to offset 70% of the ongoing operational and maintenance expenses. While the complex does not add to the property tax base and will generate only minor sales tax revenue, policymakers feel that the project enhances the quality of life in the region. Moreover, 50% matching funds are difficult to find. On the other hand, the 30% operational subsidy (the balance net cost to Highpoint City after implementing the strategy of generating 70% of the ongoing operational and maintenance expenses) represents ongoing, increased costs.

Landfill Closure: Highpoint City stopped using one of its two landfills in the past year. State law mandates extensive closure and monitoring requirements. The city has been found out of compliance and has 180 days to initiate action toward the closure and monitoring requirements. Failure to do anything results in a $10,000 penalty per day once the 180 days lapse.

Greenly Park Branch Library: The Greenly Neighborhood Association has lobbied for years for a branch library on city-owned property adjacent to the park. City staff finds that if the Greenly Park facility replacements go forward at the same time as a branch library, the larger bid package may result in a 4–7% cost reduction on all bid elements because of economies of scale. However, operational funding for books and staff associated with a new branch library are unavailable for at least three years.

Waste Water Treatment Plant and Sewer Extension for New Industrial Park: The Highpoint City Council believes in economic development and wants to open a new industrial park. Such a park will add to and diversify the tax base while stimulating other economic activity. Forecasted revenues from the industrial park after its five-year build-out will result in the payoff of the wastewater treatment plant and sewer extension needed to make this all a reality in 25 months.

Part III: Reflective Questions

After completing Parts I and II, answer the Reflective Questions on page 92.

Name _____ Date _____

Capital Budgeting Assignment Sheets

Part I: Maintenance, Repair, and Remodeling Projects

Please rank the projects in order of priority from priority 1 (highest priority) to priority 6 (lowest priority), and identify them by name. Fully explain your rationale for the recommended priority.

Priority 1   Project Name   _____

_____

_____

_____

_____

Priority 2   Project Name   _____

_____

_____

_____

_____

Priority 3   Project Name   _____

_____

_____

_____

_____

Priority 4   Project Name   _____

_____

_____

_____

_____

Priority 5   Project Name   _____

_____

_____

_____

_____

Priority 6   Project Name   _____

_____

_____

_____

_____

Part II: New Capital Assets

Please rank the projects in order of priority from priority 1 (highest priority) to priority 6 (lowest priority), and identify them by name. Fully explain your rationale for the recommended priority.

Priority 1   Project Name   _____

_____

_____

_____

_____

Priority 2   Project Name   _____

_____

_____

_____

_____

Priority 3   Project Name   _____

_____

_____

_____

_____

Priority 4   Project Name   _____

_____

_____

_____

_____

Priority 5   Project Name   _____

_____

_____

_____

_____

Priority 6   Project Name   _____

_____

_____

_____

_____

Part III: Reflective Questions

Please respond to the following questions.

1. Overall, what were the primary motivating factors that led you to rank the projects in the order you selected?

_____

_____

_____

_____

_____

_____

2. Which class of projects (maintenance, repair, and remodeling projects or new capital assets) were easier to place in priority rank? Explain why.

_____

_____

_____

_____

_____

_____

3. Provide examples of two stakeholder groups that may have a different priority of projects and explain why.

_____

_____

_____

_____

_____

_____

Exercise 10

Local Government Budget Review Analysis

Learning Objectives:

- ☑ To familiarize you with a local government budget while acquainting you with the information available.

- ☑ To task you with the responsibility to review, summarize, and critically evaluate a governmental budget from an interested citizen's perspective.

- ☑ To expose you to opportunities, challenges, and policy issues faced in the annual budget process.

- ☑ To acquaint you with the common governmental budgeting issues of staffing, performance measurement, equipment and capital improvement considerations.

- ☑ To develop critical thinking skills in evaluating governmental budgeting transparency.

- ☑ To explore various levels of reserves typically found in governmental budgeting.

Background

All governmental units must meet statutory requirements for adoption of their respective public agency budget. The difficulties of this task and sophistication of budgeting approaches varies widely. In this exercise, you have the opportunity to gain in-depth, firsthand experience in reviewing a local government budget.

Assignment

The budget analysis exercise gives students the opportunity to examine one local jurisdiction's budget in depth and critique it based on the expertise developed through the course. The assignment may be accomplished individually, or through teams of not more than three members. Each individual or team will select a proposed budget from a city or a county. You must notify your instructor of the jurisdiction selected for analysis to avoid overlap. You are responsible for accessing the budget document via the jurisdiction's website. If the jurisdiction you initially identified does not make its complete budget available on the Internet, identify an alternative jurisdiction's budget for review. Advise the instructor as soon as possible to ensure no overlap with others. Your instructor will inform you whether the Local Government Review Analysis Sheets should be completed and submitted individually or as a team.

Individual or Team Members _____

Budget Reviewed _____   Date _____

URL   _____

Local Government Budget Review Analysis Assignment Sheets

1. How is the budget organized? What are some of the major assumptions (e.g., economic growth, revenue, etc.) that are made with the budget?

_____

_____

_____

_____

_____

_____

_____

2. Does the budget document identify goals to guide the jurisdiction over the fiscal period? What are they?

_____

_____

_____

_____

_____

_____

_____

_____

_____

3. What opportunities and challenges does the document identify for the jurisdiction?

_____

_____

_____

_____

_____

_____

_____

_____

4. What approaches are recommended to address the opportunities and challenges?

_____

_____

_____

_____

_____

_____

_____

_____

5. What "policy" issues are discussed?

_____

_____

_____

_____

_____

_____

_____

_____

6. What approaches are taken to monitor, measure, and evaluate performance?

_____

_____

_____

_____

_____

_____

_____

_____

7. What type of information is presented on individual operations?

_____

_____

_____

_____

_____

_____

_____

_____

8. How are capital improvements presented and funded?

_____

_____

_____

_____

_____

_____

_____

_____

9. How are recommended staffing and equipment changes handled?

_____

_____

_____

_____

_____

_____

_____

10. Explain how the document is user-friendly or user-unfriendly.

_____

_____

_____

_____

_____

_____

_____

11. How are reserves listed and discussed in the document?

_____

_____

_____

_____

_____

_____

_____

12. Are recommended budgetary changes clear?

_____

_____

_____

_____

_____

_____

_____

13. What improvements would your team recommend? What would make the budget more understandable and user-friendly from an interested citizen's perspective? Are the jurisdiction's goals/objectives clear, and are there plans to meet them? Can you obtain a feel for how an individual agency or department is performing from the budget presentation? Is the terminology clear throughout the document? (Continue on the next page if you need more space.)

_____

_____

_____

_____

_____

_____

_____

_____

_____

_____

_____

_____

_____

_____

100

Exercise 11

Performance Budgeting

Learning Objectives:

- ☑ To define performance budgeting and outline its components and characteristics.

- ☑ To introduce benchmarking as a valuable technique to make performance comparisons with similar organizations.

- ☑ To review key elements in the design of performance measures.

- ☑ To consider the advantages, disadvantages, and challenges of perfomance budgeting.

- ☑ To challenge you to describe how you would design a performance measure for incorporation into a performance budget.

Background

Performance budgeting refers to a budgeting process that focuses on activities, their costs, and the resulting outcomes. It has a three-fold purpose. First, performance budgeting attempts to clarify what citizens receive from government for the taxes they pay. Second, when well-designed, it projects the way that resource increases and decreases influence outcomes. Third, it offers the possibility of better performance. It turns the spotlight on the mechanics of better public service delivery with expectations for improvements. These purposes are of keen interest to stakeholders (e.g., elected policymakers, managers, employees, citizens, special interest groups, and the media). Performance budgeting heralds the possibilities of more efficient, economical, and effective service improvements. Although performance data may be ignored or interpreted to suit political predispositions, the tie to activity measures supports ongoing, attentive management. This gives operating managers a baseline from which to improve and ideally motivate organizations to achieve better outcomes. It encourages strategic planning for improvement.

A performance budget explains what an organizational unit does and how well it does it. It involves segregating agencies, departments, and programs into identifiable, distinct activities. Optimally, each activity requires the design of one or more performance indicators. These indicators measure how well objectives are met. Such measures are for both internal governmental use and review by stakeholders. Specific budget detail then is assembled to generate budgets that maintain or change performance outcomes.

Performance budgeting stresses efficiency, economy, and effectiveness. Activities require careful delineation. The more sophisticated performance budgeting presentations may include the organizational mission, objectives, a functional grouping (e.g., law enforcement), an activity classification (e.g., call dispatching), workload information (e.g., calls for service), performance measures (e.g., police dispatching lapse time), and cost data per performance unit measure (e.g., cost per call dispatched). Costs include both direct expenses per performance measure as well as indirect expenses (e.g., cost per call dispatched would factor in departmental management). Performance budgeting presentations typically include data indicating unit costs and unit cost comparisons as well as a discussion of relative performance. This may be followed by some interpretation of what the data means.

Standard performance measures include (1) inputs (e.g., resources devoted to an activity), (2) workload information (e.g., measures of volume or frequency of activities over time), (3) efficiency (e.g., a ratio of inputs to outputs), (4) effectiveness (e.g., qualitative measures of how well an activity is performed), and (5) outcomes (e.g., some indication of what difference does the activity performance make). With these measures in hand, organizations often pursue benchmarking with comparable data from similar agencies. *Benchmarking* measures the performance of an organization with that of other similar agencies. Evidence that some other agency does better can motivate and propel an organization to improve efficiency. Through comparative analysis, benchmarking facilitates discovering how to improve further while rendering a realistic picture of what the next step looks like.

Design of Performance Measures

Performance measures require careful consideration. They should strive to accomplish the following:

- Focus on the service delivery mission with objectives that target definable outcomes.

- Represent timely, valid, and reliable measures. *Validity* refers to the certainty that a performance measure truly assesses what it intends to measure. *Reliability* refers to the accuracy of the performance measure to gauge consistently the same attribute over time.

- Make measuring performance and monitoring relatively easy and inexpensive while linking to desired outcomes where appropriate.

- Compare performance over time or with benchmarks through "apples to apples" comparisons with the activities of similar agencies.

- Communicate salient information to stakeholders, especially for use in decision-making, while inspiring quantitative and qualitative activity advancement(s) and a continuous improvement culture.

Integrating Performance Measures into Budgeting

A public agency integrates a performance measure into its budget after evaluation for validity and reliability and stakeholder review. In its inaugural use and periodically thereafter, an explanation of the measure bears repeating to ensure that stakeholders recall the development and attributes of the performance measure. Stakeholders may have questions or guidance for staff regarding the use of the measure.

A performance measure requires careful linking to the budget through the budget narrative with data illustrations, as appropriate. At the micro-analysis level, the full costs associated with a performance unit measure must be computed, besides understanding exactly what the measure counts. Unit costs are comprised of all direct and indirect costs. Compilation of costs usually involves accounting oversight. This oversight ensures consistent costing strategies across the organization. At the macro-analysis level, management has the responsibility of explaining how the performance measure may be employed and what it means to stakeholders. Ultimately, if the relevance of the measure is not clear to stakeholders, the performance indicator will have little credibility while consuming significant staff effort.

Monitoring and Communicating Performance Budgeting Information

After linking the performance measure to the budget, actual performance must be monitored and reported. Generally, data are collected continuously, aggregated periodically, and reported out at designated intervals. Special situations may require special off-cycle performance reports. Minimally, performance data require reporting to stakeholders as part of the annual budget process. Stakeholders will want to know if an activity exhibits significant increases or decreases. They will look to management for interpretation and recommendation concerning such developments. Stakeholders also may form conclusions independently and at variance with the information presented. This may reflect a predisposition regarding certain services and political influences beyond the presented data.

Performance Measure Development Example

Below is a hypothetical case using police dispatching as an example. It demonstrates the general development of a performance measure and its integration into the budget. Please refer back to the example to support your work in completing this exercise. Please also note that all numbers are hypothetical and for illustration only.

Government activity: Police dispatching for a City Police Department.

City Police Department Mission: To serve and to protect.

Police Dispatching Objective: To receive calls for service, screen and classify the calls, and quickly dispatch responsive resources in support of the departmental mission.

Performance measure: The lapse time between a call for service and dispatching a resource (e.g., police officer, community service officer).

Definition of a valid and reliable dispatching lapse time: A valid and reliable dispatching lapse time is defined as the time that transpires from the first ring for a call for service to the confirmation that a resource (e.g., police officer) is dispatched for action. For example, the first ring for a call for service occurs at 11:00 a.m. The dispatcher receives the call, screens the call to gather critical information, makes a call classification judgment regarding the appropriate call routing or consults with a dispatching supervisor, contacts the appropriate resource (e.g., police officer), and confirms that the contacted resource received the information for action. This series of actions may take 4.75 minutes. (Please note that all lapse times are in decimal notation so 4.75 minutes is 4 and 3/4 minutes or 4 minutes 45 seconds.)

Data collection: Lapse time data are tracked. For example, the actual dispatching lapse time for each call is recorded. Data are collected by each shift, 24 hours per day, seven days per week by the police dispatching supervisors. Supervisors calculate the range, mean, median, and standard deviations of lapse times. Data are summarized weekly by shift. For instance, the actual dispatching lapse time for the day shift may be a mean of 4.5 minutes, 5.75 minutes for the swing shift, and 4.0 minutes for the graveyard shift, with an overall mean of 4.75 minutes. Weekly summaries are compiled to develop monthly, quarterly, and annual summaries expressed in shift and overall weekly means. The overall monthly mean is used for general reporting to stakeholders.

Cost determination: All costs associated with police dispatching are captured on a regular basis to compare to the overall mean monthly dispatching lapse times and the cost determinations of similar comparison agencies. *Direct costs* will include all salary and benefit expenses for dispatchers, dispatching supervisors, dispatching manager, clerical, technical, and other personnel attributable to police dispatching. Direct costs incorporate services and supplies, equipment, and facility expenditures related to dispatching services. *Indirect costs* comprise all proportionate indirect staff, services and supplies, and equipment charges assignable to police dispatching.

Reporting intervals: Monthly, quarterly, and annual summaries are reported to the manager(s) responsible for police dispatching services regularly or by request. Management routinely shares data with policymakers up the chain of command and to stakeholders at least once a year during budget hearings.

Benchmarking: Lapse time may be measured in comparison to past time periods. Additionally, the responsible manager(s) may conduct external studies to establish other similar jurisdictions from which benchmark comparisons may be made. "Similarity" must be established carefully. It may include relative agency size, the ratio of police officers to population, the ratio of dispatchers to police officers, or some metric related to the classifications of calls for services or relative crime rate.

Performance budgeting linkage: The overall mean police dispatching lapse time per call for service is linked to the annual budget. This is accomplished by reporting the lapse time along with the overall mean cost per call for service in the budget narrative. These two numbers will be compared to previous lapse times and costs where possible. They also will be reported in comparison to similar agencies with the comparable cost per call for service.

Public policy use: The overall mean numbers will be available annually for review and comparison during budget hearings as well as upon request and for audit and evaluation purposes. Proposed resource increases and decreases will be translated into a projected public service impact for decision-making consideration. For example, the addition of five police dispatchers at a cost of $455,000 annually will reduce the overall mean police dispatching lapse time from 4.75 minutes to 3.25 minutes while the cost per call dispatched will increase by $7.50 per call. Conversely, the reduction of five police dispatchers at a savings of $455,000 annually will increase the overall mean police dispatching lapse time from 4.75 minutes to 5.75 minutes while the cost per call dispatched will decrease by $3.75 per call.

Advantages of Performance Budgeting

Performance budgeting commands great interest since it offers important information to support the budget decision-making process. The major advantages are:

- Supports stakeholders by supplying data that results in better decision making in adjusting resources to enhance efficiency, economy, and effectiveness.

- Affords an opportunity to align activity planning, budgeting, monitoring, reporting, and evaluating.

- Assists in evaluating past budget decisions while shifting resource debates from resource inputs to measurable outcomes.

- Provides a forum for discussing planned versus actual activity outcomes, leading to better control and coordination through examining activity details.

- Motivates better organizational performance through comparative analysis with similar organizations while determining best practices.

- Improves public relations by increasing transparency and accountability in reviewing budget decisions.

- Connects performance to accountability while enhancing the ability to implement managerial incentives for improved performance.

Disadvantages of Performance Budgeting

Performance budgeting also generates disadvantages. The major disadvantages are:

- Requires sufficient staff resources and expertise be allocated to install and maintain without overloading the budget process.

- Initial transition costs can be high, especially if no performance measurement elements are already in place.

- Defining an initial baseline for tracking performance is difficult.

- Linking incremental resource changes to corresponding incremental performance changes involves some interpretation of performance trends. These interpretations may not earn universal agreement.

- Connecting performance measures and actual budgetary decisions can be problematical, as performance is only one factor influencing policymakers' budgetary decisions.

- Gathering consistent data to make external comparisons with similar agencies may be impossible.

- Poor performance may be caused by reasons beyond efficiency, economy, and effectiveness, and an activity may be essential even if it is not optimally performed.

- Managers often resist performance measures when they are used to cut resources.

Performance Budgeting Challenges

Performance budgeting faces many challenges in living up to its potential to make performance more influential in budget decision making. First, despite the benefits of performance budgeting, politics and decision maker predispositions will continue to influence budgeting decisions heavily. Second, maintaining valid and reliable performance indicators and a system of cost accounting for activities over time are no easy tasks. Adequate staff resources to sustain performance budgeting will compete with the budgetary needs of other activities. Third, determining to what extent budgeting should correspond to results may inflame public controversy as politically popular program advocates feel threatened. Fourth, it may be difficult for performance successes and shortcomings to be reviewed objectively by partisan stakeholders. Fifth, public agencies must ensure that the advantages of performance measurement outweigh the disadvantages to cultivate a performance centered organization that endures over time.

Assignment

Your assignment is to use what you have learned to experiment with performance budgeting. You are tasked with logically laying out the construction of a performance measure for a specific activity and incorporating it into a performance budget. To maximize critical thinking development, your assignment should not involve a "call for service lapse time" performance measure similar to the example provided. For instance, you must avoid developing a performance measure that addresses service lapse time, such as for fire, ambulance, or animal control services. The assignment takes you through the analysis process required of performance budgeting. By engaging in the process of performance budgeting, you will better understand the opportunities and pitfalls of using performance measures. You are not required to develop actual numbers but are encouraged to use hypothetical numbers to demonstrated competency in performance budgeting concepts. Please complete the Performance Budgeting Assignment Sheets with as much detail as possible.

Name _____ Date _____

Performance Budgeting Assignment Sheets

Select a governmental activity for which you will create a performance measure. Try to provide sufficient realistic detail for your performance measure. You may want to review the performance measure development example described on pages 104–106.

1. What is the name of the government organization that incorporates your selected activity?

   _____CUSTOM_____

2. What is the governmental mission of the organization (e.g., department, division, program)?

   _____

   _____

   _____

3. What is the key objective of the activity?

   _____

   _____

   _____

4. What activity flows from the objective for which you will construct a performance measure.

   _____

   _____

   _____

5. Define a valid and reliable measure of activity performance?

   _____

   _____

   _____

6. What data will need collection, who will collect it, and when?

_____

_____

_____

_____

_____

_____

7. What are all the cost components of the activity, including indirect costs?

_____

_____

_____

_____

_____

_____

8. At what intervals will your performance information be communicated to stakeholders?

_____

_____

_____

9. How will you benchmark the performance measure?

_____

_____

_____

_____

_____

_____

10. How will you link the activity performance to the budget?

_____

_____

_____

_____

_____

_____

11. What are the proposed policy use and costs of the performance measure?

_____

_____

_____

_____

_____

_____

12. What are three advantages associated with the performance measure you propose?

_____

_____

_____

13. What are three disadvantages associated with the performance measure you proposed?

_____

_____

_____

14. Based on your narrow experience in this exercise, do you feel that the benefits from developing a performance measure outweigh the time and effort involved? How much of your conclusion is based upon the kind of activity you selected for your performance measure? Are there other kinds of governmental activities for which you might reach another conclusion about the utility of using performance measures?

_____

_____

_____

_____

_____

_____

Exercise 12

Post-Budget Adoption Unanticipated Revenue

Learning Objectives:

☑ To introduce you to the political nature of debates surrounding the allocation of budgetary resources.

☑ To develop an understanding of the conflicts created by demands and competition for budgetary resources.

☑ To expose you to various perspectives on how to address unanticipated revenue.

☑ To engage you to apply critical thinking to budget analysis and strategy when dealing with competing demands.

Background

Governmental budgeting usually unfolds in a predictable cycle. Common phases play out in a foreseeable sequence and include preparation, adoption, execution, and review and audit. Although the cycle may be characterized by extreme conflict, consternation, and stress, multiple stakeholders' interaction is an essential and healthy feature of open, democratic governance. Post-budget adoption reductions as well as augmentations may involve minor budget modifications or dramatic contentious changes creating tension, disagreement, and judgment calls among competing interests and priorities. Both also create opportunities and threats to various stakeholders in a vibrant and engaging civic environment. This post-budget adoption unanticipated revenue learning experience attempts to simulate and expose you to some of the frustrations associated with such dilemmas. Moreover, it challenges you to critically consider what skills, knowledge, and abilities are essential to public budgeting.

Scenario

University County has a $1.1 billion budget. General purpose revenues such as property and sales taxes fund $238.7 million, or 21.7% of this total. The budget was adopted in early July with a good deal of contentiousness and dozens of general employee layoffs due to constrained resources. Although no public safety employees lost their jobs, the tumultuous budget adoption hearing witnessed inadequate funding for county facilities, community development, desperately needed automation, salary and benefits settlements, and divisive split votes by the elected policymakers on almost every final budget decision.

Belatedly (after county budget adoption), the state unexpectedly restored previously reduced, discretionary funding of $12.6 million to the county. The state has not committed to maintaining the funding beyond the current fiscal year. Additionally, due to a robust real estate market, an extra unanticipated $16.0 million in property tax revenue was realized at year-end, after the budget hearing concluded. This revenue was not appropriated in the county's adopted budget. University County now faces the issue of what to do with the combined $28.6 million.

University County has set a noticed public meeting to consider what action, if any, to take with respect to the new revenues. As identified in the table below, various public representatives, county staff, and elected policymakers will present their respective ideas about what to do with the unanticipated revenues. The print media will report extensively on the process and resolution of the unanticipated revenue issues. Following the public discussion, the elected policymakers will provide direction to the county manager.

Table 1 – Stakeholder Roles

Public Representatives	Staff and Elected Policymakers
Executive Director, Taxpayers' Association	Community Center Director
President, Sierra Club	Facilities Management Director
Former Employee, Laid-off	Public Works Director
Foreman, Grand Jury	District Attorney
President, Westside Hispanic and African Amercan Coalition	Department Head, Compensation Committee Member
Manager, Law Enforcement Union	County Manager
Manager, General Employee Union	Conservative Elected Policymaker
Newspaper Reporter	Liberal Elected Policymaker

A Synopsis of the Roles

Executive Director, Taxpayers' Association

Too much of the taxpayers' hard-earned money goes to the county already. Obviously the state has overtaxed us since it finds itself with sufficient funds to restore prior county cutbacks. The surplus should be returned directly to the taxpayers, and county government should be more efficient and better managed. Further, the increased property taxes that the real estate market has produced are NOT needed. The county has developed and adopted a satisfactory budget already. It is time to reward the golden goose, the taxpayers. You DEMAND a tax rebate from the new found riches.

President, Sierra Club

Your call for permanent green space and a habitat preserve was ignored in the adopted budget. You were told that there simply was no spare funding to invest in our planet and our children's future.

The county cannot say that anymore! The newly found $28.6 million is a respectable down payment to improve our environment this year. There is no excuse now. You need to force the county to get on with it!

Former Employee, Laid Off

You assume you can return to work next Monday. When you were laid off, you were told that the county was "sorry." It lacked funds to continue your position even though deputy sheriffs received salary and benefit increases. GOOD. Money is here now. You are grateful. You plan to show-up for work on Monday.

Foreman, Grand Jury

The Grand Jury monitored the adoption of the current budget. It was messy and cantankerous. Yet, at the end of the day, a balanced budget was adopted. Now what? The swings in fortune seem to suggest the need for better financial forecasting and better intelligence on what the state plans.

Before the feeding frenzy fires up, you expect someone to guide the county to greater stability. What mechanisms can the county deploy to ensure this unanticipated revenue surprise does not happen again? What analysis is needed to ensure that the county uses the funding wisely? You want the "feast or famine" funding lurches to slow down. You need to have some answers for the public and want to see longer-term fiscal stability.

President, Westside Hispanic and African-American Coalition

Westside is a diverse, severely depressed, unincorporated portion of University County. Its population is 63% minority (38% Hispanic and 25% African-American) with the median per capita income trailing the rest of the county by 21%. The new interstate freeway lopped off Westside from the main portion of the nearest city to which annexation was planned twenty-five years ago. Westside has two freeway off-ramps in comparison with the six on the east side. One of the two exits comes to an abrupt end in a residential area since it was never completed because transportation funding dried up.

Before the interstate, Westside had modest commercial and retail development, and there was talk about a long-range industrial park and shopping mall. Since the interstate off-ramp was left incomplete, those plans have been abandoned. Additionally, the existing commercial and retail interests have stagnated with some of the "mom and pop" businesses boarded up or taken over by dingy liquor stores, beat-up bars, struggling pawn shops, and a spate of tattoo parlors.

Over the last two years, your coalition has called on University County's leadership to complete the unfinished off-ramp. Additionally, your coalition wants funding to support a sewer system upgrade necessary to attract general interest and private investment to a new industrial. park plan. The county policymakers have acknowledged the past tragedy of Westside's treatment and promised assistance to the economically depressed area. Two elected policymakers (a liberal and a conservative) share constituents in Westside. In the most recent budget adoption hearing, the policymakers considered a $4 million required match to a $40 million plan for federal and state governments to finish the off-ramp and improve arterial access to the area. Additionally, the policymakers considered a $3 million proposal for pre-design and environmental work on the sewer upgrade currently estimated to cost $17 million. Strategically, this initial work is necessary to attract other funds for the eventual project. Both of these budget proposals were dropped because of "insufficient funds" and "employee layoffs." Frustrated by the rebuff, you were told to "come back" when there was money on the table.

Well, University County, YOU'RE B-A-C-K! You want your fair share. You want a bit of social equity. You want it NOW! Further, to continue to deny this kind of basic support is nothing more than turning a blind eye to the racial injustices of the past.

Manager, Law Enforcement Union

The membership of your union feels unappreciated. Each member puts his/her life on the line every duty hour and has to grovel for comparable pay with police officers in the cities within University County. NONSENSE!

After two-and-a-half years with no contract, six months ago your union entered a three-year agreement. It keeps pace with regular county employees and comparison county law enforcement agencies, but not competing city police departments. At the same time, the contribution of law enforcement employees to their safety retirement was increased by 3% of salary, from 9% to 12%. Your union barely ratified the current agreement and did so only because a bare majority was convinced that there were no further funds on the horizon. Why is it raining dollars now? What about the Law Enforcement Union? Can the increased employee contribution to safety retirement be rescinded?

Manager, General Employee Union

As the Manager of the General Employee Union, your membership feels that the county does not respect your members. The county treats the Law Enforcement Union with kid gloves and forces cutbacks to fall on regular employees, shielding those with safety retirement and better benefits from sharing the cutback pain. One of your major units where layoffs have trimmed your dues-paying membership has just started bargaining. PERFECT! Your time has arrived. The county cannot cry poverty this time. Your union wants the positions that were cut to be restored and M-O-R-E!

Newspaper Reporter

Local government coverage has been weak lately. You specialize in conflict, controversy, and mayhem while keeping the public informed and the public servant rascals on edge. The county has experienced several tough years of troublesome budgets with much union agitation and community second guessing.

Your news organization is under financial pressure from the newspaper from an adjacent county making inroads into your customer base, especially by reporting on the county, the 800-pound public service guerilla in the area.

How do you maximize news column inches on the county's "riches," keep the public informed, ensure thorough coverage, and reassert your position with your readership that your newspaper is THE newspaper on public services?

Identify the angle(s) you will be taking in reporting the public meeting. What articles do you plan to write before the meeting? Who will you talk to, and what slant do you plan to take? What are the likely topics you plan for the newspaper immediately following the meeting? What follow-up articles do you plan to write for the week following the meeting? What kind of editorial can you outline and recommend to your editor?

Community Center Director

Your community centers are always last. You serve the elderly, the poor, and the kids. Unfortunately, while there are many of them, they usually do not make public meetings, and few advocate on their behalf. You lost two dozen employees and part-timers to balance the budget while your facility needs were deferred AGAIN. You are always the last to be considered. Is the county there yet? Is it your turn?

Facilities Management Director

New facilities can be deferred. SO BE IT! However, deferred maintenance is just foolish. For the second year in a row, the adopted budget did not fund the $3.5 million required for reroofing critical buildings. Roof leaks beget a host of more costly and dangerous building problems. Certainly, common sense and concern for employee and public safety will prevail. The $3.5 million MUST be funded to cover the current roofing crisis.

Public Works Director

Citizens and elected policymakers want pot holes fixed YESTERDAY! You have a 23-month, $13 million backlog, and no funding was available to close the gap in budget adoption. You are still assessing the new damage from the six-day storm last month that was accompanied by flooding and four hillside collapses. The harder you try, the further behind you get.

Street repair will be an issue with elections on the horizon. You cannot pretend there is adequate funding and that the public is satisfied with your response times. You also do not want to be blamed by those running for office that you are not delivering. You need to request more money than what you can realistically expect to ensure that it is "not your fault" when complaints continue. At the same time, you need to make some progress to show everyone how valuable you are, and to make some dent in the backlog. Surely, a few million dollars of the unanticipated revenue can address the more urgent needs. However, how much should you request?

District Attorney

You need to show innovative leadership with your election campaign about to take off. How can you be innovative without money?

Your department needs additional funding for your proposed cutting-edge initiatives dealing with identity theft and sexual predators. If enacted, your initiatives will place your department at the vanguard in the battle against both crimes in the region. There is also the possibility of grant funds from the state because the county has a disproportionate number of cases involving these high-profile crimes. For the identity theft unit, six investigators, two deputy district attorneys, one accountant, and three clerks are required. On a full-year basis, the staffing is estimated to run approximately $915,000. Services and supplies will run $198,750. Vehicles, computers, and office furniture add another $390,000. However, these are one-time, start-up costs.

For the sexual predator unit, six investigators, three attorneys, one victim-witness assistant, and four clerks are needed. On a full-year basis, the staffing is estimated to run approximately $1,220,000. Services and supplies will cost another $255,000. Vehicles, computers, and office furniture add another $422,000. However, these are one-time, start-up costs.

Regardless of the funding level or whether additional funds are appropriated, your pitch will warrant headlines. You will assert leadership. You cannot be blamed for not having the resources to pursue your bold, new initiatives.

H-e-l-l-o new money. ANY ELECTED POLICYMAKERS SOFT ON CRIME?

Department Head, Compensation Committee Member

MARVELOUS! Management salary and benefits are always considered after represented groups are settled. Department heads are always required to "set an example," but they are running 10–14% behind comparable counties. Yet, department heads are the line managers that have to make whatever funding there is work. You think you can make some gains now. YOU HAVE TO MAKE GAINS NOW!

Beyond additional, just compensation for department heads, the county can restore services and laid-off positions, make progress on facility needs, and finally have a pool of funds to divvy up for long-standing automation needs.

County Manager

That darn State! It dumps funds on the county unexpectedly. Coupled with the surprisingly high-assessed valuation resulting in more property taxes, the county has an amazing pot of one-time money. Or, is it one-time money? Will all the money (both state and property taxes) continue on an ongoing basis? How could your projection be so off on the property tax revenue?

What is the most prudent course of action? What analyses are required to develop a recommendation? What should be done now? What strategy makes good use of the new revenue without setting the county up for a future problem?

The policymakers will look for a recommendation. It is your job to provide analysis and recommendations. There will be great pressure to "do something." What can you recommend? What good government standards can be applied to address county needs prudently?

Conservative (Republican) Elected Policymaker

Your reelection is about one year away, and potential conservative (Republican) candidates are wondering whether they can unseat you. What should your platform be? More law enforcement is always good. What does the District Attorney really need? Can you win the next election without the support of Westside? What is the least that is required to foster Westside progress while pacifying your supporters?

The conservative constituency believes the county is not frugal enough and panders to the employee unions. The county ought to maintain and to build reserves, minimize financing costs, and concentrate on facility needs that will support population and business growth. Employees are overpaid, overbenefited, and do not work hard enough. If you do not stabilize county finances, you are history.

Liberal (Democrat) Elected Policymaker

Your reelection is about one year away, and potential liberal (Democrat) candidates are wondering whether they can unseat you. You REALLY want to support Westside. Plus, it could be a strong area for new votes with a voter registration effort.

Your constituency includes the Law Enforcement Union and the General Employee Union. You were criticized for not persuading a majority of the elected policymakers to restore cut positions in the final budget hearing, and several dozen employees were laid off.

With the growing population, all services are stretched, and there are weekly constituent complaints about the existing service levels. If you lose the support of the unions and Westside, you are history.

Assignment

This assignment can be completed either with or without an in-class role play component. If your instructor decides to include in-class role play in this assignment, you will follow the instructions for Option A. If your instructor decides not to include an in-class role play component to this assignment, you will follow the directions for Option B.

Option A: In-Class Role Play

Each student (or student group) will represent one of the roles listed under either "Public Representatives" or "Staff and Elected Policymakers." on page 114. Using the synopsis provided for a given role, each student (or student group) has 15–20 minutes to organize a three minute oral presentation about what should be done with these new revenues. Public representatives present their positions first. They are followed by county staff, and then the policymakers will speak. For Option A, the Post-Budget Adoption Unanticipated Revenue Evaluation Assignment Sheets are divided into two sections. Prior to presentations, complete the Analysis and Presentation Preparation section on pages 123–124. After all the presentations and rebuttals from the role play is done, complete the Debriefing Analysis and Discussion section on pages 125–126.

Option B: Individual or Group Written Assignment

In Option B, students will be assigned individually or as a group to represent one of the roles listed under either "Public Representatives" or "Staff and Elected Policymakers" on page 114. Using the synopsis provided for a given role, under Option B analysis and discussion will consist of written responses to similar but different questions listed on pages 127–130.

Name _____   Date _____

Option A: In-Class Role Play
Post-Budget Adoption Unanticipated Revenue Assignment Sheets

Part 1: Analysis and Presentation Preparation

Your instructor may provide more information regarding the attitudes, concerns, or individual agendas of your role (or your group role). To help you develop your argument about what should be done with these new revenues, answer the following questions from the perspective of your assigned role.

1. How do you (or how does your group) feel about the adopted budget?

   _____

   _____

   _____

   _____

   _____

   _____

2. What are your initial overall thoughts about the new found revenues?

   _____

   _____

   _____

   _____

3. What are the three strongest reasons you can present as to why the new revenues should be appropriated to address issues important to the role you play?

_____

_____

_____

_____

_____

_____

_____

_____

4. After everyone has made their initial comments, each student (or student group role) will have one minute to rebut any comment made. Be prepared with your one-minute rebuttal comment. What do you plan to say?

_____

_____

_____

_____

_____

_____

Part 2: Debriefing Analysis and Discussion

After all presentations and rebuttals, resume your identity as a governmental budgetting student, and respond to the following questions

1. Identify the three best presentations and explain what made them effective.

_____

_____

_____

_____

_____

_____

_____

_____

_____

_____

_____

_____

2. Based on the presentations, state what direction you would give to the county manager and your rationale.

_____

_____

_____

_____

_____

_____

_____

_____

_____

_____

_____

_____

126

3. In this scenario, what more do you need or want to know to make a prudent decision about what to do with the unanticipated revenue?

_____

_____

_____

_____

_____

_____

4. In this scenario, what skills, knowledge, and abilities would assist public agencies in decision making.

_____

_____

_____

_____

_____

_____

_____

Option B: Individual or Group Written Assignment

Post-Budget Adoption Unanticipated Revenue Assignment Sheets

Part 1: Analysis and Role Position

Your instructor may provide more information regarding the attitudes, concerns, or individual agendas of your role (or your group role). To help you develop your argument about what should be done with these new revenues, answer the following questions from the perspective of your assigned role.

1. Pick one role (alternatively your instructor may assign roles to avoid duplication) listed in the table on p. 114 covering "Public Representative" or "Staff and Elected Policymakers." Using the synopsis provide for each given role, compose a 500–600 word position statement about how the role you represent wants the unanticipated revenue allocated.

(continue on next page)

2. Identify two other roles from the table on p. 114, and state how your role's interest is likely to align with those roles. Articulate a strategy where these three roles work together and explain your plan for allocating the unanticipated revenue.

_____

_____

_____

_____

_____

_____

_____

_____

_____

_____

Part 2: Debriefing Analysis and Discussion

After completing Part 1, resume your identity as a governmental budgeting student and respond to the following.

1. Identify and explain what three roles you expect would provide the strongest opposition to the joint plan you articulated on the previous page.

_____

_____

_____

_____

_____

_____

_____

_____

_____

_____

2. Using your critical thinking skills and analytical ability, explain under this scenario, what other information do you need or want to make a prudent decision about what to do with the unanticipated revenue?

_____

_____

_____

_____

_____

_____

_____

_____

_____

_____

Exercise 13

A Case Study of Budgetary Obligations

Learning Objectives:

- ☑ To sharpen critical thinking skills by examining a real-life inspired case study.

- ☑ To expose you to the complexity of fiscal and budgetary decision-making in a contentious budgeting environment with numerous political interests.

- ☑ To introduce the cumulative nature of fiscal management decisions.

- ☑ To develop an understanding for the dangers associated with an overly influential leader.

Background

The Curious Case of the City of Sun-Ville

The City of Sun-Ville is a city with a population of approximately 500,000 people. It is located in one of the most prosperous counties in the country. The median yearly household income is approximately $125,000, with a per capita income of $45,000. The city, due to its location and prosperous economy, has always been an attractive destination for high earners and investors. Its residents are also known for being highly engaged in their city's governance.

In the early-1990s the city council, at the urging of the city manager, a former successful charismatic entrepreneur, embarked on a strategy to refocus the local economy from retail and tourism toward dot-com oriented businesses. This proved to be an extremely timely and lucrative decision. In particular, during the dot-com boom from 1997–2000, the city enjoyed unprecedented levels of revenue generated mostly by the new technology oriented companies. The city literally had more money than it could spend. Within this context, the city administration abandoned caution and fiscal prudence and engaged in a number of high cost capital projects. Many of these projects were not financed under the most far-sighted financing conditions. City leaders rarely considered the long-term effective cost of the financing options they were choosing, as many believed that the revenue levels would continue to grow. City employees received significant annual pay raises and multi-year labor agreements where raises became contractually "automatic." Furthermore, unions were able to renegotiate a number of improved benefits, especially in terms of future pensions. The city employees became among the best paid in the country. The city manager garnered immense levels of respect both among residents and city employees, with many considering him a hero and an economic wizard. He received all the credit for the city's economic development and quickly became known nation-wide.

Unfortunately for the city, in 2000 the Internet-bubble burst. Many of the unrealistically overvalued dot-com companies had to close shop and the city lost almost 20% of its anticipated revenues for the year "overnight." This took many by surprise, including the city manager and the city council. Everyone was convinced that the tech revolution was there for the long run. At least nobody expected that it would last only three years.

The city found itself in an extremely difficult situation. It was involved in a number of high-stakes, long term capital projects that it could not withdraw from due to contractual obligations and large sunk costs. The city residents, who became accustomed to robust services levels, were unwilling to accept any service cuts, higher fees, and tax hikes. Similarly, employee unions rejected any reductions to salary and benefit improvements they managed to negotiate just a few years back. Although the city's pension obligations were becoming a "burden," the employee unions refused to cooperate—it was not their problem. Their job was to negotiate the best terms they could for their members and they had done that admirably. The city's reserves were sufficient to maintain ongoing levels of service for another 18 months. The city could afford postponing some maintenance and some equipment purchases, but these actions would address only a meager portion of the expected budget gap for the following year. A solution was needed. It had to come quick and it had to be effective. Everyone looked to the city manager. After all, he was a legend among city managers.

The city manager did not disappoint. After reviewing the city's finances he realized that the city had a large amount of funds set aside for the city's rainy day fund. The city did not have a strict policy on the uses of the rainy day fund. The interest generated by this fund could be earmarked to address some of the employee pension obligations. These funds were conservatively invested in treasury bonds that were yielding 2.1% interest. The Internet-boom might have been over, but the rest of the economy was doing just fine. Other investment options were often able to yield return rates above 7%. It was, however, rather uncharacteristic for local government to engage in such investments. Still, the appeal of this simple solution was hard to resist. Furthermore, the city manager was fairly confident in his ability to read the market and make profitable investment decisions. Money could be generated here by making the existing money work harder. Removing the pension liabilities from the equation, relying on higher returns on investment, made balancing the budget a much more feasible task. The move was again successful. In fact, it was so successful that the city did not have to cut any services nor give up on any capital projects. Above all, the city did not have to revisit any prior labor agreements. The city's pension liabilities were addressed by aggressive investment choices. They kept growing at a steady rate, which was higher than for most other local governments. This successful move further enhanced the city manager's reputation as someone who was "head and shoulders" above his peers.

Regrettably, the city's unpleasant experience with "bubbles" did not end in 2000. Only when things seemed to be back on track and the city's future looked bright again, in 2006, the entire national economy was hit by the "housing bubble." This time around things were much more serious for the city. The economic downturn turned into the Great Recession, the worst economic downturn since the Great Depression. The city's finances took a double hit. On the one hand, the city had notable losses in its principal and also lost the interest earnings from investments that it became dependent upon for covering the pension liabilities. On the other hand, the uncovered pension liabilities grew because of the losses in stock value that resulted in a retirement system rate increase. The losses were significant. The city was looking at an approximately 40% budget gap, with as much as 30% resulting from the pension liabilities. Overall, as fiscal conditions stood, the city was looking at insolvency (inability to pay its financial and debt obligations) within two years. There was no easy solution this time. The city manager did not have a silver bullet. The city council would not have accepted any proposal (e.g., pension obligation bonds) that would have failed to address the long term financial structural issues facing the city. The overly-optimistic strategies and imprudent actions of the past became clear. But it was already too late to correct the city's fiscal path.

Amazingly, within a decade the City of Sun-Ville went from one of the most prosperous cities in the country, with a stable economy, to facing insolvency that could lead to bankruptcy. A number of what appeared at their time to be justifiable and reasonable cash management decisions ended up accumulating budgetary obligations that the city could no longer sustain. Moreover, at no point in time was the city's administration involved in any unethical behaviors nor, to the best of everyone's knowledge, did anyone have any intentions of running the city "into the ground." On the contrary, everyone involved, including the city manager, truly believed that what they were doing was in the best interest of the city and its residents.

Assignment

After carefully reading the case study, answer the questions that follow. Your instructor will indicate whether you should work individually or in groups. While you will be able to derive the answers to some of the questions directly from the reading, others will require critical thinking. You should note that since this is a case study several questions will not have "correct" answers. Although there are common lessons that everyone can learn from this case, there also can be a diverse set of perspectives when it comes to discussing the prospective insolvency.

Name (Group) _____   Date _____

Case Study Assignment Sheets

    1. Who were the main stakeholders and what are their respective interests?

_____

_____

_____

_____

    2. Which were the critical issues that brought the city to the brink of insolvency?

_____

_____

_____

_____

    3. What leadership concerns arise in this case study? What were the main risks associated with having an overly influential leader?

_____

_____

_____

_____

_____

_____

_____

_____

    4. Who should be held accountable for the current fiscal condition? Why? Are the residents in anyway responsible?

_____

_____

_____

_____

5. How could some of the erroneous decisions (and eventually the overall situation) been alleviated?

_____

_____

_____

_____

6. What are three lessons to be learned from this case study?

_____

_____

_____

_____

7. Assume that you are the newly appointed city manager for the City of Sun-Ville. What overall action plan would your propose to the city council? What do you see as your three biggest challenges and why? What are your top three proposals?

_____

_____

_____

_____

_____

_____

_____

_____

_____

_____

_____

Exercise 14

Cutback Budget Management

Learning Objectives:

☑ To define cutback budget management.

☑ To identify major factors arising from the governmental budgeting environment that influence cutback planning and management.

☑ To review the more common approaches to reducing governmental budgets.

☑ To consider cutback budgeting as both science and art.

☑ To challenge you with opportunities to construct strategies that minimize the impact of cutback budget management to public services.

Background

Cutback budget management refers to reducing governmental operations below the current level. It forces the realignment of expenses with revenues. The larger the gap between expenses and revenues the greater the cutback required to restore a balanced budget. For example, a city funded by a $100 million budget in the current year may need $104 million to function at the same level in the coming year. Such an increase may be attributable to negotiated labor contract changes, rising gasoline and utility costs, and general inflationary pressures on services and supplies. The budget increase may be needed just to maintain current operations in next year's dollars without funding any new programs, positions, or policy issues. If $104 million in revenues are not forecasted to offset these costs in the same funding cycle, a cutback budget becomes necessary.

Cutback budget management may also target a general policy theme or a specific agency or department. For instance, the federal government may de-emphasize domestic programs in favor of increased spending on national defense. In that circumstance, funding for domestic programs may be reduced, held flat, or curbed from growing at the previous rate. This would precipitate a cutback budget in domestic programs. At the local level of government, a newly elected mayor may focus her attention on spending for children's services. In this case, other departments and agencies may find that their budgets have remained the same as the previous year or even reduced.

Chief Reasons for Cutbacks

Many governmental agencies find themselves dealing with cutbacks periodically, especially during a recession. The chief reasons for cutbacks include the following:

- General economic conditions that negatively influence governmental expenses and revenues.

- Specific revenue shortfalls tied to a program or series of programs.

- Unfunded mandates from another level of government.

- Unusual or unanticipated fiscal issues resulting from war, health and safety concerns, unemployment, pension obligations, or natural disasters.

- Shifting public service demands (e.g., cutbacks in libraries, and parks and recreation in favor of more law enforcement).

- Changes in political ideology (e.g., demands for less government and more privatization).

- Efforts to reduce the size of public debt and the associated interest.

Governmental Budgeting Environment Characteristics

Several characteristics of the governmental budgeting environment influence approaches to cutback management. First, a checks and balances system rooted in governmental structures fragments control. This results in structural obstacles to timely coordinated direction. The spending/revenue gap continues and may grow while the public agency ponders fiscal adjustments. Therefore, any cutback efforts must consider ways to minimize organizational delays and inertia.

Second, government mostly provides public goods and services that are unprofitable for the private sector. Frequently, these represent goods and services that exhibit efficiency through economies of scale with costs distributed over a broad population. Consequently, market measures of efficiency and effectiveness find little use during budget hearings, as service beneficiaries argue to protect their favored programs. Further, supply and demand market rules become moot since many service recipients do not directly pay for services received and usually only one service provider exists.

Third, taxpayers generally represent "involuntary" resource providers to governments. Given the option of not paying for governmental services, many would forgo payment. The absence of the "no-pay" option fosters intense transparency and accountability pressure. Taxpayers want to know how their money is spent and who is responsible for spending it.

Fourth, incrementalism continues as the most influential government budgeting approach. It recognizes that most governmental budgets build on factors already in place. Most commonly, this would be the current year's budget or a previous year's budget. Financial plans for a subsequent year usually involve incremental additions or subtractions to that base budget. Unfortunately, incrementalism bypasses a comprehensive annual analysis of the entire budget. Depending on the spending/revenue gap, downsizing may call for overall scrutiny, performance evaluation, and radical surgery, not just an incremental adjustment.

Cutback Budget Management Planning

The severity of a cutback budget is relative. Planning strategies must be tempered by three cutback factors: size, duration, and urgency. Initially, the relative size of the budget demands determination. For example, a reduction of $100,000 from a $1 million budget may signify a devastating 10% hit with immediate layoffs and service reductions. However, a reduction of $100,000 from a $10,000,000 budget results in a 1% budget decrease. It may mean only a six-month delay in rehiring three vacant positions out of a staff of 100. Obviously, the proposed $100,000 cut poses drastically different challenges to the two budgets compared above.

Many local governments manage the "size" of departmental budgets on a "net cost" basis. This decomposes the components of a budget for management analysis. *Net cost* refers to the computation of agency appropriation minus agency revenue equals net cost. Computationally, that appears as shown in Figure 1.

Figure 1: Net Cost Computation

Agency appropriation
– Agency revenue
_____
Agency Net Cost

Discretionary, general purpose revenue (GPR) is used to cover the net cost. For example, the agency budget of $10 million may be offset with program dedicated revenues of $6 million. This leaves a net cost of $4 million for funding from GPR. Computationally, this is illustrated in Figure 2.

Figure 2: Net Cost Computation Example

$10 million appropriation
– $ 6 million revenue
_____
$ 4 million net cost

In this instance, a $100,000 reduction represents a 2.5% net cost decrease while still equaling a 1% decrease in appropriation. What merit is there to using the net cost approach? From a managerial leadership perspective, the net cost approach reminds line agency managers that the budget control point results from multiple components. Astute managers can compensate for net cost cutbacks by cutting program expenses and/or raising program revenues. Additionally, line managers learn quickly that they are accountable for timely and full receipt of program revenues. Otherwise, they may face a larger cutback that is not spread among other agencies.

The projected duration of a cutback makes a difference. A short-term cutback may be accommodated with modest actions. A one-year reduction of $100,000 on a $1 million budget could be achievable through deferring replacement of equipment, eliminating staff training, and holding off facility modifications. However, if the duration of the same cutback level is projected to continue beyond a fiscal year, other actions may be compelled. Consequently, rather than just sacrificing supporting resources and derailing facility modifications for multiple years, two staff members may require immediate termination.

Moreover, the timing of a cutback has consequences. If the organizational unit, or public agency, has several months to meet an annualized reduction goal, the path pursued may look quite different from a crisis reduction. The former may involve a cost saving reorganization or renegotiation of employee compensation by midyear. However, in a crisis situation requiring immediate cutbacks, layoffs may be unavoidable.

The crux of cutback budget management planning is that each agency's set of circumstances may be unique, even among similar agencies. Cutbacks require fact driven analysis of appropriations and revenues. This analysis must be fully informed about the cutback size, duration, and urgency. This enables evaluation of sensible solutions.

Common Cutback Budget Management Strategies

Policymakers may take the lead in providing staff direction on reconciling the spending/revenue gap. Yet, it is usually the staff that carts in the bad news and trots out a game plan to make ends meet. Cutback budget management draws from a menu of possible approaches. Options vary in response to the cutback needed and service priorities. Brief descriptions of the foremost strategies follow.

Across-the-board, general cuts. Levy across-the-board appropriation reductions (e.g., a 3% reduction to all agencies). This trims the budget without singling out any particular program, thus avoiding an angry rebuke from service beneficiaries.

Pinpoint specific percentage reductions. Target reductions selectively to particular operations (e.g., a 2% reduction to national security programs or to a state park service).

Program reductions. Eliminate specific programs, defer new programs, and reduce less popular and poorly managed programs.

Capital improvement reductions. Eliminate lower priority capital improvements, suspend previously funded projects that have not started, and defer maintenance.

Reserve level review. Reconsider reserve levels.

Personnel cost reductions. Add no new positions, eliminate temporary employees, curb overtime, enact furloughs, trim salary and benefit elements, reexamine pension plans and other post employment benefits, reorganize, and initiate a hiring freeze.

Service and supplies reductions. Restrict travel and training, minimize supply inventories, reduce/renegotiate service contracts, and restrict/reduce telephone lines.

Equipment reductions. Suspend normal replacement cycles and minimize new acquisitions.

Boost revenues. Review and consider increasing tax rates, adopting new taxes, raising contractual charges to other agencies, and assessing the appropriateness of user fees and user fee levels.

Cutback Budget Management – Science or Art?

Cutback budget management targets the balance between budget appropriations and revenues. On the one hand, to the extent that this balance involves science, quantitative analysis or mathematical approaches carry the day. Quick control over an expenditure pattern careening toward red ink takes decisive action. Reaching mathematical financial goals takes priority over a more studied appraisal of public service implications. The process reflects sober realism and sidesteps wishful thinking while avoiding any hint of chicanery. A public agency reaches the cutback through reducing expenses, increasing revenues, or some combination of the two.

On the other hand, to the extent that budget balancing involves art, operational ingenuity triumphs. Ideally, policymakers adopt governmental budgets that represent sound financial planning and that truly balance essential expenses with realistic revenues. Budget strategies reflect operational analysis, public service delivery priorities, along with tactical and strategic adjustments. Ultimately, the process strengthens the organizational core and offers opportunities for stakeholder participation while debating appropriations and revenues.

Cutback budget management fluctuates between these two extremes. In adopting a balanced budget, strategies employed must address the reasons for the cutback, the environment, and the size, duration, and urgency of the reduction.

Assignment

This exercise offers two scenarios for you to consider. Based on learning to date, you are tasked with reviewing and analyzing available information as a budget analyst. You will be asked to provide three alternative approaches to close the gap between proposed appropriations and revenues. You must then identify your recommended balancing plan and fully explain the rationale for it. Your response to both scenarios should be written on the Cutback Budget Management Scenarios Assignment Sheets on pages 145–148.

Scenario 1: City of Midland

The City of Midland, a comparatively small city with a population of 89,000, has an overall budget of $100 million. After four days of policymaker squabbling at the final budgeting hearing, the City Council tentatively expressed intent to adopt a budget that is out of balance by $405,000. The tentative budget adds seven new full-year funded positions ($504,000), a plethora of new fixed assets ($2.4 million), and an ambitious capital improvement budget ($20 million). Certain program user fees ($7.5 million) offset the budget's overall cost. Yet, these fees have not been updated for employee salary and benefit increases (the bulk of user fee cost components) for the past four years. Salary and benefit increases have averaged 4.2% annually over the past four years.

The Council has directed the City Manager to return tomorrow with three alternatives to close the gap. She has been asked to honor the Council's hard fought programmatic and policy compromises while recommending one of the budget balancing plans with a full rationale. You are the assigned budget analyst.

Scenario 2: University County

University County has a $940 million budget. Revenues of $223 million come from the state. Due to major funding issues with schools (a state responsibility), the state has made a permanent, non-program related cut of 10% to counties for the upcoming year. That means a $22.3 million permanent reduction of state revenues to University County. General purpose revenues in the county offset approximately $291 million, or 31% of the $940 million budget. These revenues grow at the rate of 5.9% per year. The county has 6,500 employees and a $74 million capital improvement budget. The average annual cost of a county employee is $72,000. The county experiences about a 7% employee turnover rate annually.

As a budget analyst on the county administrator's staff, you are assigned to develop a strategy to cut $22.3 million on an ongoing basis from the budget. Your strategy needs to be fully explained to the board of supervisors/county commissioners with targeted savings and expected impacts for each reduction component.

Name _____   Date _____

Cutback Budget Management Assignment Sheets

Scenario 1: City of Midland

Identify three alternative approaches to close the $405,000 gap between proposed appropriations and revenues based on the available information. Discuss the potential challenges or issues to each suggested approach.

Alternative 1:

_____

_____

_____

_____

_____

_____

Alternative 2:

_____

_____

_____

_____

_____

_____

Alternative 3:

_____

_____

_____

_____

_____

_____

Identify your recommended balancing plan and fully explain the rationale for it. Remember to include any assumptions, qualifications, and recommendations for future actions related to your rationale. Discuss the reasons why the city council is likely to support your proposal.

_____

_____

_____

_____

_____

_____

_____

_____

_____

Scenario 2: University County

Identify three alternative approaches to achieve the $22.3 million cut while closing the gap between proposed appropriations and revenues based the on available information. Discuss the potential challenges or issues to each suggested approach.

Alternative 1:

_____

_____

_____

_____

_____

_____

Alternative 2:

_____

_____

_____

_____

_____

_____

Alternative 3:

_____

_____

_____

_____

_____

_____

Identify your recommended balancing plan and fully explain the rationale for it. Remember to include any assumptions, qualifications, and recommendations for future actions related to your rationale.

_____

_____

_____

_____

_____

_____

_____

_____

Budget cutbacks often are required to respond to external, unpredictable factors. Explain what process you would use to improve your agency's annual comprehensive analysis to minimize an incremental approach to budgeting.

_____

_____

_____

_____

_____

Exercise 15

Postcourse Governmental Budgeting Student Survey

Learning Objectives:

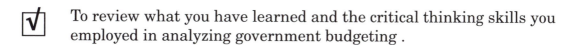 To review what you have learned and the critical thinking skills you employed in analyzing government budgeting .

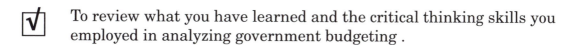 To reflect on how you might use the skills, knowledge, and abilities acquired in the course.

Background

We commenced the course with a Precourse Governmental Budgeting Student Survey. That survey sampled and explored your knowledge level of governmental budgeting prior to taking this class. This survey offers you the opportunity to review what you have learned, and to assess how this course may provide you with valuable knowledge for your current and future administrative jobs in government, nonprofit, and private enterprise organizations.

Assignment

Complete the Postcourse Governmental Budgeting Student Survey.

Name _____ Date _____

Postcourse Governmental Budgeting Student Survey

Although this is an ungraded assignment, please complete the following survey as comprehensively as possible.

1. Explain your current concept of governmental budgeting. What is a budget? Why do agencies prepare them? Why should citizens be concerned about governmental budgets?

_____

_____

_____

_____

_____

_____

2. The Government Finance Officers' Association makes budgeting best practices publicly available for review and reference. Briefly describe (1) what a *budgeting best practice* is, and (2) what value do best practices have for governmental budgeting.

_____

_____

_____

_____

_____

_____

3. What value do you see in the availability of governmental budgeting information through public agency websites? In your response, please consider the perspectives of (1) an interested citizen, (2) a governmental staff person, and (3) a non-governmental, private business or nonprofit individual.

_____

_____

_____

_____

_____

_____

_____

4. What do you consider to be critical aspects in developing governmental budgetary revenue forecasts and expenditures?

_____

_____

_____

_____

_____

_____

5. Briefly describe how you would go about evaluating (1) equiment, and (2) capital improvements for inclusion and prioritization in budget development

_____

_____

_____

_____

_____

_____

_____

_____

6. Briefly explain how you would conduct a review of a governmental budget. What would you look for?

_____

_____

_____

_____

_____

_____

_____

_____

7. Identify and explain three strategies you would employ to cutback a budget.

_____

_____

_____

_____

_____

_____

8. How can you use course learning in your current and/or future positions?

_____

_____

_____

_____

_____

_____

9. What contribution do you see governmental budgeting skills, knowledge, and abilities making to your career?

_____

_____

_____

_____

_____

_____

Exercise 15 Postcourse Governmental Budgeting Student Survey